CONTEMPORARY & TRADITIONAL
RESOURCES FOR WORSHIP LEADERS

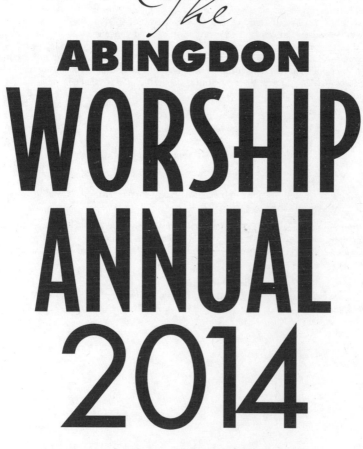

The
ABINGDON
WORSHIP
ANNUAL
2014

EDITED BY MARY J. SCIFRES & B. J. BEU

Abingdon Press
Nashville

THE ABINGDON WORSHIP ANNUAL 2014
CONTEMPORARY AND TRADITIONAL RESOURCES FOR WORSHIP LEADERS

Copyright © 2013 by Abingdon Press

This book is printed on acid-free paper.

Library of Congress Cataloging-in-Publication Data

978-1-4267-5825-6

All Scripture quotations unless noted otherwise are taken from the Common English Bible (CEB) © 2011. Used by permission.

Scripture quotations marked NRSV are taken from the New Revised Standard Version of the Bible, copyright 1989 by the Division of Christian Education of the National Council of the Churches of Christ in the United States of America. Used by permission. All rights reserved.

Liturgies marked UMH or that refer to *The United Methodist Hymnal* are based on *The United Methodist Hymnal,* copyright 1989 by The United Methodist Publishing House. Used by permission.

13 14 15 16 17 18 19 20 21 22—10 9 8 7 6 5 4 3 2 1

MANUFACTURED IN THE UNITED STATES OF AMERICA

CONTENTS

CONTENTS

INDEXES

ONLINE CONTENTS

The following materials are found only in the Abingdon Worship Annual 2014 *section at* www.abingdonpress.com/ downloads. *Instructions on how to view these materials in your browser or download them to your computer, are available at the site. PLEASE NOTE: This file is password protected; please see page vii for the password.*

INTRODUCTION

As we celebrate our tenth anniversary with this edition of *The Abingdon Worship Annual*, we offer our gratitude to our readers. Your many hours of prayer, discernment, planning, and preparation transform the words we have shared through this resource into amazing moments of worship and spiritual nurture for your congregations. Thank you!

We know that worship is a precious and intimate time in the life of every congregation. When your congregation entrusts you with the preparation and planning of worship, they grant you a great honor. For these last ten years, you have granted this honor to us, along with our many contributing authors, as you have allowed us into your ministry of worship planning and preparation.

Each year, we have adapted and changed *The Abingdon Worship Annual* as we strive to meet your worship planning needs. But as always, you will find words and ideas to focus each week's worship service alongside prayers and litanies for congregational participation. Included with this book is Internet access to full texts for each worship service on the related site abingdonpress.com/downloads (click on the link to *The Abingdon Worship Annual 2014,* and when prompted, enter the password: worship2014). This will allow you to import printed prayers and responsive readings directly into your bulletins for ease of use and printing. Look for some surprises in the online edition as well: hymn and song suggestions, worship website suggestions, and a full compendium of ideas for celebrating New Year's Eve, or Watch Night, in worship.

In *The Abingdon Worship Annual 2014*, you will find the words of many different authors, poets, pastors, laypersons, and theologians. Some names you will recognize; others will be new to you. All have prayerfully studied the lections for their given worship days, focused on themes for those days, and composed words within a suggested flow for worship.

Since the contributing authors represent a wide variety of denominational and theological backgrounds, the words before you will vary in style and content. Feel free to combine or adjust the words within these pages to fit the needs of your congregation and the style of your worship services. (Notice the reprint permission for worship given on the copyright page, p. ii, of this book.)

This *Worship Annual* contains words for worship, placed in an order of worship, for each Sunday of the lectionary year, along with suggestions for many of the "high" holy days. At your request, we no longer substitute a lectionary Sunday with an adjacent "high" holy day. So, now you can easily choose to celebrate Ascension Sunday or 7th Sunday of Easter, All Saints Sunday or the scheduled Sunday of the Ordinary Season.

Each entry provides suggestions that follow an order of service that may be adapted to address your specific worship practice and format. Feel free to re-order or pick and choose the various resources to fit the needs of your worship services and congregations. Feel free, as well, to follow the suggested flow to ease your own task of planning and ordering worship.

Each entry follows a specific thematic focus arising from one or more of the week's scriptures. This focus, along with corresponding Scripture imagery, is then carried out through each of the suggested prayers and litanies for a given worship service (and in the song suggestions available in the online edition). For those who are working with contemporary worship services or prefer more informal words, alternative ideas for those settings are offered for each service as well, at the end of the entry. Each entry includes a Call to Worship and Opening Prayer, Prayer of Confession and Words of Assurance, Responses to the Word, Offertory Prayer, and Benedictions. Communion Resources are offered in selected entries (see the Communion Prayer and Liturgies Index to locate these). Additional ideas are also provided throughout this resource. We have ordered each day's suggestions to fit the Basic Pattern of Christian Worship, reflecting a flow that leads from a time of gathering and praise, into a time of receiving and responding to the Word, and ending with a time of sending forth. The Praise Sentences and Gathering Words fit the spontaneous and informal nature of many non-traditional worship styles and easily fit into the time for gathering and praise. They are often designed for use in worship without a printed program or bulletin. However, some readers find the Gathering Words or Unison Prayers helpful as written words of "centering" to be printed in a worship handout or bulletin. Use the words offered here in whatever way best serves your congregation's spiritual needs, and please remember to give copyright and author credit!

Although we do not include specific worship rubrics (or instructions) for each service, worshipers are often more comfortable with spoken or written instructions. Don't hesitate to begin a Prayer or Call to Worship by offering simple instructions, such as:

Please join in the Call to Worship.
Let us worship God as we speak together.
Let us praise God.
Please pray with me.
Let us pray together.
If you can make this prayer your own, please join me in unison prayer.
Let us come to Jesus Christ, confessing our sin and our need.
Please join me in praising God.

Remember that body language communicates as effectively as verbal language. Raise your arms as you invite those who are able to stand. Bow your head (keeping close to the microphone) as you invite others to pray with you. Smile and speak energetically when offering Words of Praise. Most of all, worship God as you invite others to do so. As we lead the people of God in worship, the congregation needs to experience the authenticity of our love for God.

USING THE WORSHIP RESOURCES

As you work with this year's resource, here are some comments to help in making the fullest possible use of it. **Calls to Worship** are words that gather God's people together as they prepare to worship God. Often called "Greetings" or "Gathering Words," these words are typically read responsively. However, they can be read antiphonally (back and forth) between two readers or two groups within the congregation. **Gathering Words** or **Praise Sentences** serve this function in more contemporary settings, but may also serve as Calls to Worship in a traditional or blended setting. As with all responsive readings, think creatively as you plan your services. While it is simplest to have a single leader read the words in light print, with the congregation responding by reading the words in bold print, it is often effective to have several people, or even groups of people, lead these calls. Using the choir, a youth group, or a small prayer group, adds variety and vitality to your services. Some congregations enjoy responding to one another: women to men, right side to left side, children to parents. Experiment with a variety of options, and see how these words might be most meaningful in calling your congregation together to worship the Holy One.

Gathering Words and **Praise Sentences** are offered here to assist pastors and worship leaders who are new to the art of leading less formal worship, sometimes called Contemporary Worship. Leaders who find speaking extemporaneously difficult will find these entries particularly helpful when leading worship. The words given are usually listed as call and response (light print for leader, bold for worshiper), but can just as easily be read by one or two worship leaders for congregations with worshipers who are hesitant to participate verbally.

In this resource, **Gathering Words** tend to use simpler language than Calls to Worship and are more repetitive in nature, for ease of participation. You may copy these gathering words onto an overhead transparency to help your congregation read responsively without being tied to a bulletin. If your congregation does not care to read words aloud, consider using two leaders to speak in "call and response" format. Or, allow the song team or band members to act as responders to the worship leader, echoing the call-and-response tradition of African American Christians.

While many of the **Praise Sentences** provided in this resource are easily spoken by one leader, using the call-and-response format is an option. In praise settings, worshipers are often willing to respond back in echo form, repeating the words or phrases spoken by the worship leader. Echoing the same words and phrases several times can be highly effective. The **Praise Sentences** in this resource are intended to free you to lead in an informal style, where appropriate.

Opening Prayers in this resource are varied in form, but typically invoke God's presence in worship. Some are more informal than others, and some are more general than formal invocations. Many can be adapted for use later in the worship service, if that suits your needs. For simplicity's sake, we have grouped them all into the category of "Opening Prayers."

Prayers of Confession and **Words of Assurance** follow many different formats. Likewise, **Prayers** take many forms in this resource. Some are unison, some responsive, and almost all are adaptable for either format. Prayers need not be spoken in unison, but may be spoken by a single leader or led by a small group. Some prayers may even be used as Opening or Closing Prayers. In all cases, we have sought to provide words that can easily be spoken by a large congregation in unison.

Litanies or **Responsive Readings** offer additional ways of speaking together in worship. Certain scriptures and themes elicited such provocative litanies that we felt called to include them. We hope you will find this a helpful addition. Again, think creatively as you decide how these **Responsive Readings** are used in your service of worship: in unison, by a worship leader alone, or in a call-and-response format. When using these prayers and responsive readings, you may use any title you deem appropriate in your worship bulletins.

Benedictions, sometimes known as "Blessings" or "Words of Dismissal," are included in each entry. Some work best in call-and-response format; others seem more appropriate as a solitary blessing from the worship leader. Choose a format best suited to your congregation: in unison, by a worship leader alone, or in a call-and-response format.

In response to requests from many of our readers, we have provided **Communion** liturgies as well, each written specifically to relate to the thematic and scriptural focus of the day. Some follow the pattern of the Great Thanksgiving; others are Invitation to Communion or Communion Prayers of Consecration for the celebration of the Eucharist.

Although you will find *The Abingdon Worship Annual 2014* an invaluable tool in planning worship, it is but one piece of the puzzle for worship preparation. For additional music suggestions, you will want to consult *Prepare! An Ecumenical Music and Worship Planner,* or *The United Methodist Music and Worship Planner,* each containing lengthy listings of lectionary-related hymns, praise songs, vocal solos, and choral anthems. As you plan lectionary-based worship, preachers will find *The Abingdon Creative Preaching Annual 2014* extremely useful. Worship planners and preachers can rely upon this collection of resources to provide the words, music, and preaching guidance to plan integrated and coordinated worship services.

All contributions in *The Abingdon Worship Annual 2014* are based upon readings from the *Revised Common Lectionary*. As you begin your worship planning, we encourage you to spend time with the scriptures for the day, reflecting upon them thoughtfully and prayerfully. Review the thematic ideas suggested in this resource and then read through the many words for worship provided that speak to the theme in reflection of scripture. Listen for the words that speak to you. Let this resource be the starting point for your worship planning. As the Spirit guides you and God's word flows through you, we pray that your worship planning may be meaningful and fulfilling, for both you and your congregation. Trust God's guidance, and enjoy a wonderful year of worship and praise! We offer our prayers and blessings as you seek to share God's word and offer experiences of the Holy Spirit in your work and worship!

Mary J. Scifres and B. J. Beu, Editors
The Abingdon Worship Annual
beuscifres@gmail.com

Learn more about workshop and training opportunities through Mary Scifres Ministries at www.maryscifres.com.

JANUARY 1, 2014

New Year

Mary J. Scifres

COLOR

White

SCRIPTURE READINGS

Ecclesiastes 3:1-13; Psalm 8; Revelation 21:1-6a; Matthew 25:31-46

THEME IDEAS

Contrasts are everywhere in today's readings: birth and death, mourning and dancing, Alpha and Omega, beginning and end, hungering and feeding, and even sheep who give and goats who neglect. As the new year begins, we face the contrast of our hopes and dreams against the backdrop of the realities we face. Contrasts are everywhere in our lives. Even as 2013 comes to an end, 2014 arrives with new possibilities. Even as we resolve to pray faithfully, eat healthily, and give generously, we are tempted to ignore soul, body, and community in the wake of old habits and long-settled choices. Choosing one path may depart from other paths, but scripture reminds us that these separate paths are somehow connected, even the paths of life and death. Even in the Christmas season, we are shown the Easter truth that life can arise in the midst of death.

INVITATION AND GATHERING

Call to Worship (Ecclesiastes 3, New Year)

After weeks of rushing and responding,
  this is a season to stop and reflect.
Even when sounds and lessons overwhelm us,
  this is a season to listen and learn.
Even when sorrow and loneliness abound,
  this is a season to laugh and love.
Even when life disappoints us,
  this is a season to hope and believe.
In this season of possibilities, Christ walks with us
through the marshes of entrenched obstacles.
  We are not alone.
Walk into the new year with God.
  This is a season of new beginnings.

Opening Prayer (Ecclesiastes 3, Matthew 25)

God of new beginnings and faithful endings,
  walk with us into this new year.
Show us the majesty of your presence,
  that we may walk forth in light and hope.
As we listen to your word,
  help us learn the lesson of contrasts.
Help us recognize your presence
  in every aspect of life—
      birth and death,
      tears and laughter,
      losing and finding,
      waging war and establishing peace.
God of both sheep and goats,
  guide us to walk with you into this new year
      with hearts full of expectant longing. Amen.

PROCLAMATION AND RESPONSE

Prayer of Confession (Matthew 25)

Forgive us, O God,

 when we stand with the goats,
  pretending not to see you
   when faced with hunger
    or the agony of grief.
Forgive us, O God,
  when we neglect the needs around us
   and the possibilities of hope
    we would bring to others
     if we chose to share our gifts.
Forgive us, O God, forgive us.
(A time of silence may follow.)

Words of Assurance (Revelation 21, Matthew 25)
Truly I tell you, that the end of the goats
  need not be our ending.
For Christ is our righteousness,
  and God is making all things new,
   wiping away tears and offering new beginnings
   with each new day.
Come, beloved, inherit God's realm,
  even as we create it here on earth!

Passing the Peace of Christ (Ecclesiastes 3)
For everything, there is a time and a season: a time to love
and a time to hate, a time for war and a time for peace.
This is a time for love and peace, and for reconciliation
and forgiveness in the body of Christ. Let us not go into
the new year with feelings of hate or with words of anger
and resentment. Come, let us forgive the wrongs of the
past, and share the peace of Christ, just as Christ has
shared God's peace and forgiveness with us.

Introduction to the Word (Ecclesiastes 3, Matthew 25)
Listen to the contrasts of God's truth . . . hope arises from
despair, laughter co-exists with sorrow, sheep walk alongside goats, rich walk alongside the poor. All have equal
opportunity to serve God and God's people among us.
Listen for the word of God.

Response to the Word (Revelation 21, Matthew 25)
God of new beginnings and faithful endings,
   walk with us into this new year.
Open our eyes to see you
   in everyone we meet.
Open our hearts to welcome others
   with the same love we would greet Jesus.
Live in us,
   that we might shine light
     into shadows of sorrow,
   that we might offer hope
     to those hungering for mercy and joy.
With faith in new beginnings, we pray this day. Amen.

THANKSGIVING AND COMMUNION

Invitation to the Offering (Matthew 25)
Among us are people who suffer hunger and thirst. Our neighborhoods are filled with people who are lonely and in need of our welcome. Our towns hide people who are dressed in rags and are in need of warm clothing. Jesus is among us: here, on the street, in our town, in our world. Do you see Christ? Do you hear the need? Let us walk as Christ's sheep and give to God's world.

Offering Prayer (Matthew 25)
Bless these gifts, guide our actions,
   and strengthen our souls, Holy One:
     that all who are naked
      may find clothing and shelter,
     that all who are hungry and who thirst
      may find nourishment and refreshment,
   and that all who are lonely and imprisoned
     may find love and companionship.
This is our offering.
This is our prayer.
This is your word, living in us
   and going forth from us
     to care for your world, O God.

Blessing of the Love Feast (Matthew 25, New Year, Love Feast)

(In the Methodist tradition, many congregations celebrate a Moravian love feast as part of a Watch Night service or alongside John Wesley's Covenant service. In addition to this unison prayer, which is intended for use in a love feast, see additional resources for this service and website references in the New Year Resources appendix online.)

God of abundant love,
    bless these gifts of food and drink,
        that even as we are nourished,
            we may nourish others.
Help us share the abundance
    of love and generosity
        that flow in our lives.
As we taste the sweetness of this offering,
    may we be a sweet offering for your world.
As we share in the refreshing gift of drink,
    may we pour ourselves freely with love and grace
        into the lives of neighbors, friends,
            and strangers.
God of abundant love, bless us,
    that we may be a blessing to others.

(See January 1 in The Abingdon Worship Annual 2013 *for a Great Thanksgiving and Communion Prayer for traditional communion services.)*

SENDING FORTH

Benediction (Matthew 25)

The home of God is among us, even now.
    May we bring God's home
    to all who are homeless and alone.
The love of God is in us, even now.
    May we bring God's love to those we meet,
    even the despised and the hated.
The life of Christ is ours, even now.
    May we be light and life

for a hurting and dying world.
The power of the Spirit blesses us, even now.
**May we live to bring a happy new year
to everyone we meet.**

CONTEMPORARY OPTIONS

Gathering Words (Ecclesiastes 3, New Year)
The past year is ending. A new year is beginning.
Some people are laughing and rejoicing.
Others are crying and filled with grief.
This is a time of old and new, gladness and sorrow,
    despair and hope.
As we face the contrasts of the turning of the year,
    may we behold the grace of God
    that is always with us.

Praise Sentences (Ecclesiastes 3, Revelation 21, New Year)
This is a time to laugh and sing!
God's love is always with us!
This is a time to rejoice and praise!
God's joy is always with us!
This is a time to celebrate the new year!
God's Spirit is always with us!

JANUARY 5, 2014

Second Sunday after Christmas
Mary J. Scifres

COLOR
White

SCRIPTURE READINGS
Jeremiah 31:7-14; Psalm 147:12-20; Ephesians 1:3-14; John 1:(1-9), 10-18

THEME IDEAS
This seldom-celebrated Sunday of the lectionary year always falls between New Year and Epiphany and usually gets lost in the shuffle of those two celebrations. However, the readings offer a different perspective on Christmas, particularly for those congregations that do not celebrate Christmas Sunday with the reading from John 1. Focusing on John's birth poem, this day celebrates light and life, as we move into the season following Epiphany.

INVITATION AND GATHERING

Call to Worship (John 1)
The light of the world is here.
  Christ is among us now.
The light of life is ours.
  Christ's life brings grace and truth.
The light of God shines anew.
  Christ's light brings love to a weary world.

—OR—

Call to Worship (John 1)
In the beginning was the Word.
And the Word was with God.
And the Word was God.
Christ is our Word, from the beginning.
The light of God shines in the darkness.
Christ is our Light, shining with glory.
Christ has come, full of grace and truth.
In the beginning was the Word.
And the Word was with God.
And the Word was God.

Opening Prayer
Light of the world,
    shine upon us this day.
Enlighten us with your wisdom,
    and free us with your grace.
Embolden us with your confidence,
    to proclaim for all to hear
        that your light shines in the darkness,
            and the darkness has not, will not,
                and cannot overcome it.
In the light of your truth, we pray. Amen.

PROCLAMATION AND RESPONSE

Prayer of Confession (John 1)
Light of the world,
    shine upon us this day.
Shine with truth into the darkest places of our lives,
    that we may face the reality of our fears
        and our sins.
Shine with grace into the shadows of our hearts,
    that we may know your forgiveness and love.
Shine with clarity into our world,
    that we may recognize sinful situations
        and oppressive systems.

Shine with truth and justice into our communities,
   that your light may overcome the darkness
      of hatred and violence.
Shine with compassion into our lives,
   that we may radiate with your brightness—
      forgiven and reconciled,
      refreshed and restored,
         shining for all the world to see.

Words of Assurance (John 1)
The light of Christ shines and shines and shines.
The light of Christ shines so brightly
   that the darkness has not, will not,
   and cannot overcome it.
Rejoice, for the light of our forgiveness
   comes from the Light of the world!

Passing the Peace of Christ (John 1)
Share light and life, my friends, as we pass the peace of
Christ with one another.

Introduction to the Word (John 1)
The true light that gives light to all is coming into the
world. Look...listen...for the Word is with us now.

Introduction or Response to the Word (John 1)
Do you see the light of Christ?
Do you hear the word of God?
Christ is among us now.
God is speaking to us still.
In the world, making the world, loving the world,
   God is with us, here and now.

Response to the Word or Benediction (John 1)
In the beginning was the Word.
   At the end is the Word.
In the middle is the Word.
   In all of life is the Word.
The Word was with God.
   And the Word is God.

9

The Word was with us, and is with us.
Thanks be to God for this marvelous gift!

THANKSGIVING AND COMMUNION

Invitation to the Offering (Ephesians 1, John 1)
Blessed with every spiritual blessing, we are the people
of God, the church of Christ. May we share our blessings
as we give our tithes and offerings, our lives and our love.
Come, let us bless others as we have been blessed. Let us
shine light for the world, as light has shined upon us.

Offering Prayer (John 1)
God of love and light,
 shine through the gifts we bring to your table.
Shine through our lives and our ministry,
 that your radiance may bring hope and life
  to a world shadowed by sorrow and need.
In the light of your generous love, we pray. Amen.

Great Thanksgiving (Christmas)
(See The United Methodist Book of Worship, *pp. 56–57, for a
Great Thanksgiving focused on Christmas readings and John 1.)*

SENDING FORTH

Benediction (John 1)
Christ's life is our light.
 May we shine as light for God's world!
Christ's love is our truth.
 May we go forth as love in God's world!

CONTEMPORARY OPTIONS

Gathering Words (John 1)
Light and life, love and grace … Christ is all of these.
Light and life, love and grace … we are all of these.

—OR—

Gathering Words (John 1)

The light of God is shining.
Christ is our light!
The light shines, even in the darkest places.
Christ is our light!
The true light lives among us.
Christ is our light!
The light of God is full of grace and truth.
Christ is our light!
Thanks be to God.

Praise Sentences (John 1)

The light shines in the darkest night.
Christ's light is beautiful and bright.
The light shines in the darkest night.
Christ's light is beautiful and bright.

JANUARY 6, 2014

Epiphany of the Lord
Mary J. Scifres

COLOR
White

SCRIPTURE READINGS
Isaiah 60:1-6; Psalm 72:1-7, 10-14; Ephesians 3:1-12; Matthew 2:1-12

THEME IDEAS
God's wisdom, in its rich variety, is incarnate in Christ Jesus. Such wisdom is offered to all who would seek to rule with justice and righteousness. This theme is seen most clearly in the visitation of the wise men from the East, but is also echoed by the psalmist, who reminds us that wisdom is the greatest gift a ruler can receive when given the responsibility of leadership. The epistle adds that the mystery of God's wisdom is revealed not only in Jesus' life and ministry, but also in the work and ministry of the church (Ephesians 3:10). This ancient news—taught through the law, the prophets, and the psalmist, and lived out in Jesus' ministry—reminds us that godly rulers judge with righteousness, and lead by defending the cause of the poor, delivering the needy, and crushing the oppressor. In the political arena, this is light at its brightest, and glory at its most radiant.

INVITATION AND GATHERING

Call to Worship (Isaiah 60, Psalm 72)
Arise with hope, and shine with love!
Shine forth with the wisdom of God!
Arise with mercy, and shine with grace!
Live in righteousness and peace.
Arise with justice, and shine with compassion.
Radiate the brightness of Christ!

Opening Prayer (Isaiah 60, Ephesians 3, Matthew 2)
God of kings and rulers, paupers, and peasants,
shine upon your people with wisdom and truth.
As the wise men opened their treasure chests
to the infant Jesus and his family,
open our hearts this day,
that we may bask in your radiance
and worship in the presence
of your compassion and love.
In your glorious name, we pray. Amen.

PROCLAMATION AND RESPONSE

Prayer of Confession (Isaiah 60, Matthew 2)
God of wisdom and truth,
forgive us when we choose to walk in darkness
rather than in your radiant light.
Shine through our doubts and despair,
that we may trust in the hope
of your mercy and grace.
Shine into our selfishness and sense of entitlement,
that we may live as people of generosity
and compassion.
Be with us now, Christ Jesus, and shine upon us!
May the light of your birth
shine into our darkest sorrows,
and gather us into your holy presence
this Christmas season and in the year ahead. Amen.

Words of Assurance (Isaiah 60)

Arise, shine, for Christ's light has come!
The glory of the Lord has arisen upon us,
 and Christ's mercy has restored us
 with forgiveness and grace.
Arise, shine, for Christ's light is shining upon us now!

Passing the Peace of Christ (Isaiah 60)

Arise, shine with peace and love for all who are gathered
here!

Introduction to the Word (Ephesians 3)

The mystery of God is revealed in the hearing and in the
living of Christ's gospel of love. Listen well, that you may
hear the wisdom of God revealed in its rich variety, made
known to those with ears to hear.

Response to the Word or Benediction (Isaiah 60, Psalm 72)

Lifting up our eyes, we see the light of Christ.
Lifting up our hearts, we hear the truth of love.
Lifting up our spirits, we discern God's wisdom.
Lifted up, we are ready to go forth as God's people,
 with justice and compassion for all.

THANKSGIVING AND COMMUNION

Invitation to the Offering (Isaiah 60, Matthew 2)

Come into Christ's light with your gifts. They need not be
gold or precious oils. Gifts of love and compassion are the
greatest treasures of all.

Offering Prayer (Psalm 72, Matthew 2)

King of justice and righteousness,
 receive these gifts,
 that they may be treasures for a world in need.
Receive the treasures of our hearts and our lives—
 treasures poured out before you,
 that we may bring light and life to all.

The Great Thanksgiving (Epiphany)
The Lord be with you.
And also with you.
Lift up your hearts.
We lift them up to the Lord.
Let us give thanks to the Lord our God.
It is right to give our thanks and praise.

It is right, and a good and joyful thing,
    always and everywhere to give thanks to you,
    almighty God, creator of heaven and earth.
In ancient days, you created us in your image,
    and invited us to be reflections of your glory.
When we fell short and dimmed the brilliance
    of your wisdom shining through us,
    you held our hands and we left your garden
    and ventured into all the corners of the earth.
From ancient times, down through all the ages,
    you have trusted us, redeemed us from sin,
    saved us from oppression,
    and proclaimed our place as your people.
In the dark wilderness of days gone by
    and days yet to come, you shine as a pillar of light,
    and invite us to shine with your wisdom and truth.

And so, with your people on earth,
    and all the company of heaven,
    we praise your name
    and join their unending hymn, saying:
    Holy, holy, holy Lord, God of power and might,
        heaven and earth are full of your glory.
    Hosanna in the highest. Blessed is the one
        who comes in the name of the Lord.
    Hosanna in the highest.

Holy are you, and blessed is the light of the world,
    Christ Jesus.

15

From a humble beginning to a violent death,
    Jesus shone with the light of your wisdom and love.
His ministry and teachings stand even today,
        as beacons of justice and righteousness,
        in a world darkened by oppression and sin.
Through Jesus' humble beginnings,
        you invite us to humble ourselves and to live simply.
Through Christ's patient love and unfailing grace,
        you shine on us with forgiveness and deliverance,
        that we, your redeemed children,
        might shine in your world, as signs of hope and love.
On the night when Jesus faced the darkness,
        he offered signs of light as he took the bread,
        gave thanks to you, broke the bread,
        and gave it to his disciples, saying:
        "Take, eat; this is my body which is given for you.
        Do this in remembrance of me."
When the supper was over, and as Jesus prepared
        to face his darkest fears, he took the cup,
        gave thanks to you, and gave it even to disciples
        who would betray and reject him, saying:
        "Drink from this, all of you; this is my life
        poured out for you and for many, in covenant
        for the forgiveness of sins.
        Do this, as often as you drink it,
        in remembrance of me."

With joy and gratitude, we break this bread
        and share in this cup, remembering the many ways
        the wisdom of God is revealed to us
        in the breaking of bread and in the stories
        of Jesus' presence in our lives.
And so, in remembrance of these, your mighty acts,
        and your wisdom revealed in Jesus Christ,
        we offer ourselves in praise and thanksgiving,
        as signs of light and life, wisdom and truth,

in union with Christ's offering for us,
as we proclaim the mystery of faith.
Christ has died.
Christ is risen.
Christ will come again.

Communion Prayer (Epiphany)
Pour out your Holy Spirit on our fellowship,
that we may be your light for the world.
Pour out your Holy Spirit
on these gifts of bread and wine,
that we may be filled with your wisdom
and nourished by your compassion.
By your Spirit, make us one with Christ,
one with each other,
and one in ministry to all the world,
until Christ comes in final victory,
and we feast at the heavenly banquet.
Through your Son, Jesus Christ,
with the Holy Spirit in your holy church,
all honor and glory is yours, almighty God,
now and forevermore. Amen.

SENDING FORTH

Benediction (Isaiah 60, Ephesians 3)
Arise, shine, for Christ's light has come.
Christ's light goes with us now.
Arise, go forth, for you are Christ's lights.
May we shine with wisdom and love.

CONTEMPORARY OPTIONS

Gathering Words (Matthew 2, Christmas)
Where is the child? Where is the Christmas hope?
In tinsel and trees? Not so much.
In parties and pictures? Not there either.
Look to the child of love,
the Christ who awaits our treasures.

Look to the child of wisdom,
　　the Christ who reveals God's wisdom,
　　justice, and righteousness.
Look to the child of light,
　　who shines with compassion and love.
There is the child. There is the Christmas hope.

Praise Sentences (Isaiah 60)

Arise, shine, Christ's light has come!
We rejoice in God's glorious hope!
Arise, shine, Christ's light has come!
We rejoice in God's glorious hope!

JANUARY 12, 2014

Baptism of the Lord

Mary J. Scifres

COLOR
White

SCRIPTURE READINGS
Isaiah 42:1-9; Psalm 29; Acts 10:34-43; Matthew 3:13-17

THEME IDEAS
The Spirit of God brings reconciliation and justice. Today's scriptures remind us that the blessing of God's Spirit in baptism is a call to ministry—a ministry of justice and reconciliation. By inviting the Gentiles onto the path of discipleship, Peter reminds us that this path is for all who wish to follow Jesus' way of justice and reconciliation. God's Spirit brings both blessing and challenge, for baptism is both an invitation of gracious love and a call to discipleship.

INVITATION AND GATHERING

Call to Worship (Isaiah 42, Matthew 3)
Come, servants of God.
   God's Spirit has called us here.
Come, servants of Love.
   God's Spirit calls us to justice and peace.
Come, followers of Christ.
   God's Spirit calls us to reconciliation and love.

Come, beloved children of God.
God's Spirit is a blessing for all.

Opening Prayer (Isaiah 42, Matthew 3)
Spirit of God,
    descend upon us this day.
Bless us with your presence,
    that we may know you more fully
        and bless others with your love and grace.
Guide us on this covenant journey,
    that we may bring sight to the blind
        and release to the captives.
Renew us with the breath of new life,
    that we may live as children of love
        and seekers of justice.

PROCLAMATION AND RESPONSE

Prayer of Confession (Isaiah 42, Matthew 3)
Gracious One,
    wash over us with your baptism
        of forgiveness and reconciliation.
When we neglect justice;
    when we cause strife;
        when we walk away from your path of discipleship,
            forgive us.
Wash over us with your baptism
    of forgiveness and reconciliation,
        that we may be made whole again. Amen.

Words of Assurance (Isaiah 42, Matthew 3)
See, the former things have passed away.
In Christ, new hope is declared;
    grace springs forth;
        and reconciliation with God
            is ours for the asking.
Rejoice, for in Christ we are forgiven
    and made new.

Rejoice, beloved, for God is well pleased
    to offer us forgiveness in grace and love.

Passing the Peace of Christ (Matthew 3)

As forgiven and reconciled children of God, let us share
signs of reconciliation with one another as we pass the
peace of Christ.

Response to the Word (Isaiah 42, Acts 10, Matthew 3)

We are the Lord's servants, God's beloved children.
    God's Spirit is with us now.
We are Christ's sisters and brothers, the family of God.
    We will offer sight to the blind
    and release to the captives.
We are witnesses to Christ's mercy and grace.
    We will extend our arms to embrace everyone
    in God's reconciliation and love.
We are God's servants, called to justice and love.
    God's Spirit calls us forth.

THANKSGIVING AND COMMUNION

Offering Prayer (Isaiah 42, Matthew 3)

Mighty God of love and justice,
    send your Spirit upon these gifts
        of personal treasure and worldly wealth;
    send your Spirit upon our gifts
        of time and talent.
Breathe into us and into these offerings
    the newness of your life,
        the faithfulness of your justice,
            and the hope of reconciliation and peace.

SENDING FORTH

Benediction (Isaiah 42, Psalm 29)

May God bless you with strength and hope.
May God grace you with justice and peace.
Go with these precious gifts of God!

21

CONTEMPORARY OPTIONS

Gathering Words (Isaiah 42, Matthew 3)

Christ's light is shining.
God's Spirit has called us here.
Christ's presence is all around us.
God's Spirit has called us here.
Christ's peace calls us forward.
God's Spirit has called us here.
Christ's light is shining with justice and hope.
God's Spirit has called us here.

Praise Sentences (Psalm 29)

Glory to God, glory and might!
Glory to God, glory and might!
Glory to God, strength and beauty!
Glory to God, strength and beauty!
Glory to God, glory and might!
Glory to God, glory and might!

JANUARY 19, 2014

Second Sunday after the Epiphany

B. J. Beu

COLOR

Green

SCRIPTURE READINGS

Isaiah 49:1-7; Psalm 40:1-11; 1 Corinthians 1:1-9;
John 1:29-42

THEME IDEAS

Can one person make a difference? Today's scriptures answer with a resounding, "Yes!" Isaiah proclaims for all Israel to hear: "Listen to me... pay attention, you peoples!" (49:1 NRSV). The psalmist confesses that the Lord has "put a new song in my mouth, a song of praise for our God" (40:3). Paul preaches that he was "called by God's will to be an apostle of Jesus Christ" (1 Corinthians 1:1). Andrew hears of Jesus from John the Baptist and says to his brother: "We have found the Messiah" (John 1:41). It is easy to see the impact of Isaiah, the psalmist, and Paul, but what of Andrew? What difference did he make? Andrew brought his brother Simon to Jesus—a brother whom Jesus renames Peter, a brother whom Jesus calls the rock. If we follow God's call, we can all make a difference, if only by inviting others onto the journey with us.

INVITATION AND GATHERING

Call to Worship (Isaiah 49, Psalm 40)

Listen, O coastlands.
Pay attention, you people of God.
God has called each of us
to be a light to the nations.
The Lord has put a new song in our lives,
a song of praise to our God.
We will sing of God's salvation.
We will shout of God's faithfulness.
Listen, O coastlands.
Pay attention, you people of God.
God has called each of us
to be a light to the nations.

Opening Prayer (Isaiah 49, 1 Corinthians 1)

Holy One, may our lives be like polished arrows
    in the quiver of your searching love;
may our intentions be pure,
    and may our words be true,
        as we proclaim your saving ways.
Call us once again, O God,
    as you called Isaiah and Paul before us.
Call us to deliver news of your goodness and mercy
    into a world of brokenness and pain,
        that your salvation might reach
            the ends of the earth,
                and your mercy might extend
                    to the farthest shores. Amen.

PROCLAMATION AND RESPONSE

Prayer of Confession (Isaiah 49, 1 Corinthians 1, John 1)

Merciful God, it is easy to succumb to despair—
    fearing we will never really make a difference;
    worrying we are not worthy of your love;
    regretting that we fail to live up to your call.

Ease our minds and heal our broken spirits
    with the balm of your never-failing love and grace.
Remind us, Loving Presence,
    that though we may not speak words of hope
        like the prophet Isaiah,
    or preach words of encouragement
        like the apostle Paul,
    we can still invite others onto the journey with us,
        as Andrew invited his brother Simon
            to meet Jesus and find the Messiah.
When others ask us if we have found the Lamb of God,
    give us the courage and the faith to boldly proclaim:
    "Come and see!" Amen.

Words of Assurance (Isaiah 49, Psalm 40, 1 Corinthians 1)

The One who called Isaiah before he was born,
    the One who put a new song in the psalmist's mouth,
    calls us and sanctifies us to be the saints of God.
The One who polishes us like an arrow,
    and who fills us with light, is faithful,
    bringing us into fellowship with our brother,
    Christ Jesus.

Response to the Word (Isaiah 49, Psalm 40, 1 Corinthians 1)

Listen, O coastlands.
Pay attention, you people of God.
    God shines within us,
    that we might be a light to the nations.
Sacrifice and burnt offerings
are not pleasing to our God.
    We will look within our hearts
    and follow the law of God written there.
Listen, O coastlands.
Pay attention, you people of God.
    God shines within us,
    that we might be a light to the nations.

THANKSGIVING AND COMMUNION

Invitation to the Offering (Isaiah 49, Psalm 40)

What does God require of us, and with what shall we come before the Lord? It is not with sacrifice and burnt offerings, but with hearts filled with praise and lives bent on justice. In joy and thanksgiving for the tender mercies of our God, may today's offering be a sign of our commitment to bring God's justice and compassion to our communities and to the larger world.

Offering Prayer (John 1)

Lamb of God,
    you blessed us with water and the Spirit,
      that we might know fullness of life;
    you call us to be saints and a light to the nations,
      that others might be brought
        to the dawn of your glory.
May our gifts and our giving
    reach the very ends of the earth,
      that those who struggle to see your light
        might be helped to discover your glory
          for themselves. Amen.

SENDING FORTH

Benediction (Isaiah 49, Psalm 40, 1 Corinthians 1)

Go forth with a new song in your heart.
    We go in the love of the One who strengthens us.
Go forth and answer the call that stirs within you.
    We go in the fellowship of Jesus Christ.
Go forth as the saints of God.
    We go in the community of the Holy Spirit.
Go forth to bring hope to the ends of the earth.
    We go to shine God's love for all to see.

CONTEMPORARY OPTIONS

Gathering Words (Isaiah 49, Psalm 40)

Can you hear God's call?
    Where is God speaking?

God is speaking far and near.
God is speaking with the earth and in the sea.
   Now you're talking in riddles.
   What is God saying?
God is speaking of light and life.
Christ is calling to one and all.
   Surely not to us?
   Doesn't God only call saintly people?
The Spirit has gathered each of us here to listen....
Listen, listen, listen.
   What is the Spirit saying?
We are the ones called to bring light to the nations.
   We are the ones called to be the saints of God.

Praise Sentences (1 Corinthians 1, John 1)
   All praise to God,
   who is our light and our salvation.
      All praise to the Lamb of God,
      who is our hope and our strength.
   All praise to the Spirit,
   who is our fortress in times of trial.
      Christ is here.
      Come and see!

JANUARY 26, 2014

Third Sunday after the Epiphany
Joanne Carlson Brown

COLOR
Green

SCRIPTURE READINGS
Isaiah 9:1-4; Psalm 27:1, 4-9; 1 Corinthians 1:10-18; Matthew 4:12-23

THEME IDEAS
Epiphany is the season of light, and these texts proclaim the light that has come into the world. This light has come particularly to those who sit in darkness: the darkness of exile, the darkness of division, the darkness of suffering, or the darkness of ignorance to the true word of God. And when the light dawns on their minds and souls and hearts, it calls forth a response—rejoicing, renewed commitment to God, walking in God's ways, and even following a stranger into an unknown, uncertain future.

INVITATION AND GATHERING

Call to Worship (Isaiah 9, Psalm 27, Matthew 4)
To those who sit in darkness, light has dawned.
To those who dwell in gloom and despair,
God's glorious presence has appeared.

God is indeed our light and our salvation.
We will follow, unafraid,
where God and Jesus lead us.
Let us worship our God of light and promise.
Let us celebrate the hope and joy of our salvation.

Opening Prayer (Isaiah 9, Psalm 27, Matthew 4)
God of light and love,
    we come this morning
        with eyes stinging from the brightness
            of your glory.
We have become so accustomed to the darkness,
    that your radiant light sometimes overwhelms us.
Open our eyes to the light of your dawn,
    that our souls may be flooded
        with love and mercy and joy.
Open our hearts to receive your message
    of comfort and peace and security,
        that we may find rest
            in your loving, protective presence.
Open our spirits to follow the path you put before us,
    that we may lead lives committed to your Way. Amen.

PROCLAMATION AND RESPONSE

Prayer of Confession (Isaiah 9, Psalm 27,
1 Corinthians 1, Matthew 4)
God of our light and our salvation,
    sometimes we prefer to live in dakness,
        embracing the safety and anonymity
            of the shadows;
    sometimes we delight in our divisions,
        believing we are better than others;
    sometimes the yoke of our calling feels too heavy,
        and we seek to slip out from under the bar
            across our shoulders.
Forgive our fear.
Forgive our aversion to the light.

29

Forgive our unresponsiveness to your call.
Forgive our willful blindness and deafness to the Way.
Help us know deep in our souls
    that you are our light and our salvation,
        our joy and our wonder,
            our very life.
Hear us as we cry aloud in our need. Amen.

Words of Assurance (Psalm 27)
Our God of light and love hears us when we cry aloud.
We have nothing to fear.
Know that this God of light
    wraps us in comforting arms,
      lifts us from the darkness of our guilt and sin,
      and forgives us once and for all.
Know that we will dwell in safety in God's house,
    now and forevermore.

Passing the Peace of Christ (Psalm 27)
Greet one another with these words: "The God of light and love and salvation surrounds you with joy and peace."

Prayer of Preparation (Isaiah 9)
Open the eyes of our hearts, O God, to the dawning light of your words of love and salvation.

Response to the Word (Isaiah 9, Psalm 27, Matthew 4)
O God,
    for the light your words bring to our understanding,
    for the hope your words bring to our fear,
    for the guidance your words bring to our path,
      we give you thanks.

THANKSGIVING AND COMMUNION

Invitation to the Offering (Isaiah 9, Psalm 27)
Light has dawned in our lives and in our world. We are called to share that light, and to speak words of comfort

and calling in a world shrouded still in gloom and darkness. Our offering will enable this community to be a beacon of light to those caught in the darkness of suffering
and wandering.

Offering Prayer (Isaiah 9, Psalm 27, Matthew 4)
What can we offer in thanksgiving
    for the gift of light and life and love
        we have received from you
           and from your Beloved Community
              here on earth?
We offer our all:
    our resources, our energy, our time, our very selves
        to answer your call and to follow without fear.

SENDING FORTH

Benediction (Isaiah 9, Psalm 27, Matthew 4)
Go forth bathed in the light and love of God.
Go forth to join with Jesus to proclaim the good news
    of this love and light.
Go forth empowered by the Spirit
    to live the Way with courage, conviction, and joy.

CONTEMPORARY OPTIONS

Gathering Words (Isaiah 9, Psalm 27)
Hey you . . . yes you over there . . . and you over there . . .
    you sitting in darkness.
Don't you know the light is dawning?
Can't you feel it on your face and in your soul?
Get up, embrace the light, shout and sing for joy!
Let's worship this blazing God of light and love.

Praise Sentences (Psalm 27)
God is our light and our salvation!
We'll never be afraid again!
Sing and make joyful music to our amazing God!
God is our light and our salvation!

31

FEBRUARY 2, 2014

Fourth Sunday after the Epiphany

Mary J. Scifres

COLOR

Green

SCRIPTURE READINGS

Micah 6:1-8; Psalm 15; 1 Corinthians 1:18-31;
Matthew 5:1-12

THEME IDEAS

The theme of reversal emerges in today's readings. In Matthew's Beatitudes, Jesus proclaims blessing and reversal of fortune to the lowly and meek, the very ones the world takes for granted. Paul reminds the Corinthians that the foolishness of the cross, however antithetical to the world's understanding, is the wisdom and power of God. God and Micah dialogue about the sad history of rejection and conflict between God and the Israelites, and then Micah reminds his listeners that reconciliation emerges not from "right offerings" or perfect worship, but rather from righteous living—through justice, compassion, and humility. None of these reversals is a new prophecy, but rather a reversal of the misconceptions we tend to live by—misconceptions born of relying on ourselves and on worldly wisdom for guidance.

INVITATION AND GATHERING

Call to Worship (Micah 6, Matthew 5)
With what shall we come before God this day?
With love and justice,
with compassion and kindness.
With what shall we worship the Lord this day?
With humility and mercy,
with faithfulness and righteousness.
Come into God's presence, not as perfect beings,
but as people of hope and blessing.
Blessed are the poor in spirit.
Blessed are the meek and the merciful.
Blessed are the sorrowful and those who dream
of peace and righteousness.
Bring your dreams. Bring your sorrows.
For all are welcome here!

Opening Prayer (Micah 6, Matthew 5)
O Holy One,
   born of the assurance
     that our worship need not be fancy,
      our offerings need not be huge,
       and our lives need not be perfect,
        we come seeking your blessing.
May we see your presence blessing our lives
   and the lives around us.
Bless us all, O God,
   that we may walk humbly with you,
     seeking justice and loving kindness,
      every day of our lives.
Bless us, Source of Blessing,
   that we may bless your world.

PROCLAMATION AND RESPONSE

Prayer of Confession (Micah 6, 1 Corinthians 1, Matthew 5)
With what shall we come before God this day?
With humble hearts and honest words.

34

Merciful God, your mercy seems foolish
and your grace unfathomable.
We do not always walk with you,
let alone walk humbly with you.
Forgive us when we stray.
In a world that teaches power and selfishness,
we do not always perceive what is just,
let alone strive to bring it about.
Forgive us when we turn away.
In a time when cruelty seems to be a spectator sport,
we are not always the face of compassion
or the voice of kindness.
Forgive us when we neglect a neighbor in need
or cause hurt in another's life.
Bless us with the gift of mercy,
that even as you forgive us,
we can forgive ourselves and others.
In grace and gratitude, we pray. Amen.

Words of Assurance (Micah 6, 1 Corinthians 1)

O, my people, remember the saving acts of God, the mercy of Christ, and the foolishness of the cross that is a gateway to enduring compassion and eternal life.
In this foolishness of God, you are forgiven!
Thanks be to God!

Passing the Peace of Christ (1 Corinthians 1)

Let us boldly embrace the foolishness of God over the wisdom of the world by sharing signs of love and peace, even with those who have wronged us and those we have never met. Let us pass the peace of Christ.

Response to the Word (Matthew 5)

Blessed are those who hunger and thirst
for righteousness, for they will be filled.
Blessed are we when we hunger and thirst
for justice and righteousness,
for we will be filled!
Blessed are the pure in heart, for they will see God.

Blessed are the peacemakers,
for they will be called children of God.
**Blessed are we when our love is pure
and we live in peace, for we are living in unity
with God and with one another!**
Blessed are the poor in spirit,
for theirs is the kingdom of God.
Blessed are the meek, for they will inherit the earth.
**Blessed are we when we are humble and meek,
creating God's realm on this good earth!**

THANKSGIVING AND COMMUNION

Invitation to the Offering (Micah 6, Matthew 5)
We, in the fullness of our humanity, are the offering that
God requires. Come into God's presence with humility
and compassion, with justice-seeking and loving-kindness
in your hearts. As the offering is collected, not only give of
your worldly treasures, but give of yourself in prayerful
offering to God, that you may see where you are blessed,
and where you may in turn bless others. Come, let us
bring our best offerings to God.

Blessing the Offering (Micah 6, Matthew 5)
Blessed are these offerings:
    offerings of peace and justice,
    offerings of love and compassion,
    offerings of kindness and mercy.
Blessed are the givers of these offerings:
    givers of peace and justice,
    givers of love and compassion,
    givers of kindness and mercy.
Blessed are we who are entrusted by God
    to share God's gifts with the world!

Great Thanksgiving (Micah 6, Matthew 5)
The Lord be with you.
And also with you.

Lift up your hearts.
We lift them up to the Lord.
Let us give thanks to the Lord our God.
It is right to give our thanks and praise.

It is right, and a good and joyful thing,
always and everywhere to give thanks to you,
almighty God, creator of heaven and earth,
bringer of justice and righteousness.
In ancient days, you created us in your image,
and invited us to be reflections
of your presence in the world.
When we fell short and wandered far
from your path of justice and love,
you held our hands and walked with us
in humility and compassion.
You called us to be your people,
and invited us to walk humbly beside you.
Even when we turned away,
you continued to walk with us,
calling us back to your path of justice and love,
through the proclamation of your law,
the words of your prophets,
and the wisdom of your poets and storytellers.
In the fullness of time, you sent your Son, Jesus Christ
to reveal your gracious presence in the world,
and to invite us onto the journey anew.
You anoint us with your blessing and trust,
and call us to bless your world
with your love and compassion, justice and truth.

And so, with your people on earth,
and all the company of heaven,
we praise your name
and join their unending hymn, saying:
Holy, holy, holy Lord, God of power and might,
heaven and earth are full of your glory.

**Hosanna in the highest. Blessed is the one
who comes in the name of the Lord.
Hosanna in the highest.**

With joy and gratitude, we break this bread
and remember the many times
when Jesus blessed his disciples
in the breaking of the bread.
In remembrance, we will take and eat this bread
and reflect on your blessed presence
which fills our souls and leaves us satisfied.
With joy and gratitude, we fill this cup
and remember the many times
when Jesus poured out his love and compassion.
In remembrance, we will drink from this cup
and reflect on your blessed presence
which overflows in our lives
and invites us to bless others as we are blessed.

And so, in remembrance of these
your mighty acts of love and grace,
we offer ourselves in praise and thanksgiving
as humble servants, walking with you
in justice and compassion,
as we proclaim the mystery of faith.
**Christ has died.
Christ is risen.
Christ will come again.**

Communion Prayer (Micah 6, Matthew 5)
Pour out your Holy Spirit
on our fellowship,
that we may be blessed with your love
and your grace.
Pour out your Holy Spirit
on these gifts of bread and wine,
that they may nourish us
with your wisdom and truth.

Guide us in your Spirit,
   that we may walk humbly by your side.
Make us one with Christ in compassion and mercy,
   one with each other in justice and kindness,
      and one in ministry to all the world,
         until Christ comes in final victory
            and we feast at your heavenly banquet.
Through Jesus Christ,
   with the Holy Spirit in your holy Church,
      all honor and glory is yours, almighty God,
         both now and forevermore. Amen.

Giving the Bread and Cup
*(The bread and wine are given to the people, with these or other
words of blessing.)*
The life of Christ, revealed in you.
The love of Christ, flowing through you.

SENDING FORTH

Benediction (Micah 6, 1 Corinthians 1, Matthew 5)
Go forth, foolish followers of God.
   We go with the power of Christ's compassion.
Go forth, foolish believers in justice.
   We go seeking justice and peace.
Go forth, foolish lovers of kindness.
   We go with the foolish grace of God.

CONTEMPORARY OPTIONS

Gathering Words
With what shall we come before our God?
   We come with burdens and worries.
With what shall we come before our God?
   We come with scattered thoughts and emotions.
With what shall we come before our God?
   We come with hectic schedules and deadlines.
With what shall we come before our God?
   We come with friends and family,

with strangers and neighbors.
With what shall we come before our God?
We come with offerings and ministries,
with time and talents.
With what shall we come before our God?
We come with thankful hearts
and yearning souls.
With what shall we come before our God?
We come with a desire to seek justice,
and to sow kindness.
Come, my friends, let us walk with our God
in humility and love.

Praise Sentences (Matthew 5)

Blessed are we by God's mercy and grace!
Blessed are we by God's love and compassion!
Blessed are we by God's mercy and grace!
Blessed are we by God's love and compassion!
Praise God for blessing us this day!

FEBRUARY 9, 2014

Fifth Sunday after the Epiphany

Mary J. Scifres

COLOR

Green

SCRIPTURE READINGS

Isaiah 58:1-9*a*, (9b-12); Psalm 112:1-9, (10); 1 Corinthians
2:1-12, (13-16); Matthew 5:13-20

THEME IDEAS

Combining the salt and light passages from Isaiah and
Matthew sheds a new perspective on the meaning of discipleship. Followers of Christ fulfill the law and the
prophets by answering Isaiah's call to justice as the path
to divine connection. When the Israelites turned their back
on justice and compassion, they lost their connection with
God. But in receiving the judgment that justice must be
the center of a godly life, we are all given the good news
that God is with us in our justice-seeking and our
compassion-giving. Our light breaks forth like the dawn
and shines brightly upon the hill for all to see. Our lives
are salty with Christ-like love and mercy when we feed
the hungry, house the homeless, and break the yokes of
injustice and oppression. Let the light shine!

INVITATION AND GATHERING

Call to Worship (Isaiah 58)
Shout to the Lord . . .
with justice and love.
Cry out to God . . .
for righteousness and truth.
Sound the trumpet . . .
of compassion and grace.
Shout to the Lord . . .
with justice and love!

—*OR*—

Call to Worship (Matthew 5)
Salt and light, justice and love,
you are the salt of the earth.
Bring your flavorful gifts to God!

Opening Prayer (Isaiah 58, Matthew 5)
Light of the World,
shine upon us,
that we may glimpse
your wisdom this day.
Love of all creation,
flow through us,
that we may be filled
with your compassion and grace.
Flavor and spice of life,
salt us with your truth,
that we may spread
your justice and love
into all the corners of the earth.
In the light of your love, we pray. Amen.

PROCLAMATION AND RESPONSE

Prayer of Confession (Isaiah 58)
We call upon you, O God,
crying out for the strength
to walk in your ways
and to live in your truth.

When we neglect the needs
  of the hungry and the homeless,
    turn our faces to see the face of poverty
      in our midst.
When we ignore oppression and injustice,
  turn our attention to notice the needs of a world
    struggling for righteousness.
When we cry out for you,
  but do not cry out for your people in need,
    speak to us of compassion and kindness,
      that we may return to your ways
        and live in your truth.
Forgive our neglect.
Forgive our inattention.
Forgive our selfish cries.
Guide us to water your world
  with compassion and love
    as you spring forth in our lives
      with compassion and grace.

Words of Assurance (Isaiah 58, Matthew 5)
Christ guides us continually,
    blessing and strengthening us with grace
      to walk in God's ways.
Receive the gift of forgiveness,
  that you may water the world
  with the same mercy and compassion
  you have experienced in Christ Jesus!

Passing the Peace of Christ (Matthew 5)
You are the light of the world! Let your light shine as you
turn to one another and offer signs of light and peace.

Response to the Word (Isaiah 58, Matthew 5)
Pour your holiness upon us,
  that we may be inflamed with your Spirit
    of charity and love.
Salt us with a passion for justice,
  that we may go forth in courage and strength
    to break the bonds of oppression and poverty.

Enlighten us with wisdom,
   that we may create a world
      where righteousness and compassion
         spring forth like living waters,
      where the rich and poor alike are fed,
      where none shall be afraid.

THANKSGIVING AND COMMUNION

Invitation to the Offering (Matthew 5)
   You are the salt of the earth. Bring your flavorful gifts
   to God!

Offering Prayer (Isaiah 58, Matthew 5)
   God of light and love,
      shine through these offerings,
         that our love may radiate
            throughout the world.
   Make bright the hope of justice and mercy
      in places of darkness and fear.
   Guide our paths,
      that we may always be lights of compassion
         for a world in need.

SENDING FORTH

Benediction (Isaiah 58, Matthew 5)
   You are the light of the world!
   You are the salt of the earth!
   Go forth with compassion, mercy, and grace.
   Go forth with confidence, strength, and hope,
      shining for all to see!

CONTEMPORARY OPTIONS

Gathering Words (Isaiah 58, Matthew 5)
   Salt and pepper, light and dark, love and justice....
   With these diverse gifts, we flavor the world with hope,
      color creation with new possibilities,

and infuse this earth with a glimpse of God's realm.
Come, bring your flavorful presence
  into this time of worship!

Praise Sentences (Isaiah 58, Psalm 112)

Shout out for the oppressed and the poor.
  We sing of God's love and justice!
Lift your voices for the needs of the hungry
and the homeless.
  We sing of God's love and justice!

FEBRUARY 16, 2014

Sixth Sunday after the Epiphany

J. Wayne Pratt

COLOR

Green

SCRIPTURE READINGS

Deuteronomy 30:15-20; Psalm 119:1-8; 1 Corinthians 3:1-9; Matthew 5:21-37

THEME IDEAS

Today's readings challenge us to choose life. As the church, we are called to focus on what God's kingdom requires, what it blesses, and how the worshiping community is to live out its distinct calling to be the body of Christ. Moses reminds the people of their covenant to worship God alone and to walk in the ways of the Lord. Paul helps the congregation at Corinth to understand and reframe its views of leadership, particularly in relation to understanding the gift of growth that comes through the power of the Spirit. In Matthew's Gospel, Jesus begins to move his followers from their assumptions about the ways of God: "You have heard that it was said..." to the ways of the gospel: "but I say to you...." The teachings of Jesus confront us with choices, each carrying its own unique consequences. Jesus calls us to choose the practices that will bring God glory and honor.

INVITATION AND GATHERING

Call to Worship (Psalm 119)

Happy are those who walk in God's ways.
**Blessed are those who observe God's
commandments.**
Faithful are those whose eyes are fixed
on righteousness.
**Joyful are those whose hearts are filled
with praise.**
Come, let us love the Lord our God.
**We come to worship the One who leads us
in the ways of life.**

Opening Prayer (Deuteronomy 30, Matthew 5)

Holy Spirit, guide us as we walk in faith,
and guard us against the powers
that would draw us away from your love.
Help us live according to your commandments,
that we might live long in the land
you have prepared for us.
Prompt us to seek you with our whole heart
and guide us to walk in your ways,
that we may carry out the vows
of the covenant we share.
May our words and deeds
bring life and faith to others,
as we hold fast to the gift of faith.
Be near us each and every day,
and bless us with your light,
that our days may be filled with grace. Amen.

PROCLAMATION AND RESPONSE

Prayer of Confession (Deuteronomy 30, 1 Corinthians 3)

Loving God, you call us to walk in your ways,
observe your commandments,
and love you as you have loved us.

You offer us a community of abundant blessing,
    with rich soil to promote dynamic growth.
Yet we often turn away from you
    to satisfy our own wants and desires.
We forsake the way of love and forgiveness,
    giving in to petty jealousies and quarreling,
      and surrendering our lofty ideals
        to our baser inclinations.
Forgive us, O God.
When we flee from your embrace,
    draw us into community with you
      and with one another.
Shower us with the cleansing waters of humility,
    that we may reclaim our purpose
      and find nourishment and growth
        in labors of love
          to bring your kingdom in our midst.

Words of Assurance (Deuteronomy 30, 1 Corinthians 3)

God is alive and at work nurturing our growth,
    nourishing our needs, and reconciling us
    to one another.
God hears the confessions of our hearts
    and forgives generously, sharing love with all
    who follow in God's ways.
It is through God's amazing grace that we are forgiven.
And all God's children respond:
Thanks be to God!

Response to the Word (Matthew 5)

O God, send your Spirit upon us and light our path,
    that we may travel the road
      you have prepared for us.
Having heard your scriptures proclaimed,
    and your word revealed,
      enable our hearts and minds
        to more fully understand
          your goodness and your grace.

Help us break free from ideas that no longer bring life,
 that we may embrace the life-giving
  work of your Spirit.
Challenge us to forsake paths that ask little of us,
 and help us resist the evils
  and temptations of this world,
   that we may truly follow the way
    of kingdom living. Amen.

THANKSGIVING AND COMMUNION

Offering Prayer (1 Corinthians 3)

Gracious God,
 as we present these offerings,
  may we be reminded of the many blessings
   you have shared with us as individuals,
   and as a community of believers.
You have fed us with the milk of your grace,
 and have nurtured us with a love
  that knows no limits or boundaries.
May our sharing this day
 reveal our priorities and our promises,
  for we belong to you and offer you our gifts,
   that they may be used
    in mission and in ministry
     to bring glory to you, our Creator,
      Redeemer, and Sustainer. Amen.

Invitation to Communion (1 Corinthians 3)

As we gather at the Lord's table, all are welcome. Having a common purpose, we receive growth from the love of God, and nurture and nourishment from the body and blood of Christ Jesus. At this table, we are redeemed by God, reconciled to one another, and called to labor in God's fields, where love and forgiveness are sown. The table is ready; the meal is prepared. Come, be fed, and savor the feast of the Lord!

SENDING FORTH

Benediction (Deuteronomy 30)
As we journey out into the world,
    may each of us walk in the light of God's ways,
    striving to be blameless and just.
May our hearts be vessels of God's love
    and may the Lord bless us in the land
    that we are entering.
Hold fast. Do not be led astray,
    and may the love of God
    be yours this day and forevermore.
Go now in peace. Amen.

CONTEMPORARY OPTIONS

Gathering Words (Deuteronomy 30)
Love your God,
and walk in God's ways.
    We will love God,
    and walk in God's ways.
Love your God,
and hold fast to God in everything you do.
    We will love God,
    and walk in God's ways.

—*OR*—

Gathering Words (Psalm 119)
Happy are those who seek God in all things,
who turn from wrong and walk with God.
    Happy are those who know God's love,
    and live with joy.
Happy are those who share praise
with a heart of pure love.
    Happy are those who know God's love,
    and live with joy.

Praise Sentences (Deuteronomy 30)
Choose life! Choose God!
Live in God's love!
God's way is good!
Hold fast to God!

(Mary Petrina Boyd)

FEBRUARY 23, 2014

Seventh Sunday after the Epiphany

B. J. Beu

COLOR
Green

SCRIPTURE READINGS
Leviticus 19:1-2, 9-18; Psalm 119:33-40;
1 Corinthians 3:10-11, 16-23; Matthew 5:38-48

THEME IDEAS
Leviticus urges us to be holy, for God is holy. Paul takes
this a step further by saying that because God's Spirit
dwells within us, we are God's temple. And because God
is holy, we are holy temples. We just need to start to act-
ing like it. The psalmist suggests we do this by following
God's precepts. Jesus suggests we do this through love—
a love that makes us perfect, even as God is perfect. Such
perfection is attained by loving our enemies and returning
good for evil—for God makes the sun rise on the evil and
the good, and sends rain on the unrighteous and the righteous (Matthew 5:45). For Jesus, perfection is found in
love's perfection.

INVITATION AND GATHERING

Call to Worship (Leviticus 19, Psalm 119,
1 Corinthians 3, Matthew 5)
God calls us to be holy, for God is holy.
God's precepts lead us into life.

Christ calls us to be perfect,
as God, our heavenly Mother and Father, is perfect.
**We are made perfect by loving our enemies
and returning good for evil.**
The Spirit calls us to be holy,
for we are temples of God.
**God's Spirit dwells within us.
In the Spirit we find our true home.**
*(This reading leads well into the hymns "Take Time to Be Holy"
and "Holy, Holy, Holy.")*

Opening Prayer (Psalm 119, Matthew 5)
Holy God, teach us your ways of life and death.
When we are wronged,
help us turn the other cheek
without anger or resentment.
When we are asked to give to those in need,
help us offer what we can
without judgment or bitterness.
Show us how to love our enemies
and repay evil with kindness,
that we might be perfect
even as you are perfect. Amen.

PROCLAMATION AND RESPONSE

Prayer of Confession (Leviticus 19, 1 Corinthians 3, Matthew 5)
Author of righteousness,
it is hard to be a holy people.
You call us to love our neighbor
as we love ourselves.
But sometimes it makes us wonder:
Have you ever met our neighbors?
You call us to show no partiality,
for you make the sun to shine
on the evil and the good;
and you cause the rain to fall
on the righteous and the unrighteous.

But sometimes it makes us question:
Do you really know what you're asking of us?
You assure us that your Spirit resides within us,
that we are your holy temple,
but we confess to feeling tired and empty.
Forgive us, gracious God.
In your righteousness, give us life,
that we may truly live
and know love's perfection. Amen.

Words of Assurance (Matthew 5)

The One who makes the sun to shine
on the evil and the good,
the One who sends rain
on the righteous and the unrighteous,
shows no partiality and loves us all
with a fierce passion.
Have no fear, beloved of God.
Love one another as God has loved us,
for our sins are forgiven!

Response to the Word (Psalm 119)

Teach us your ways, O Lord,
that we may live by your statutes
with hearts filled with joy.
Give us understanding,
that we may follow your paths
all the days of our lives.
We have longed for your words of life, O God.
In your righteousness, give us life. Amen.

THANKSGIVING AND COMMUNION

Offering Prayer (1 Corinthians 3, Matthew 5)

Eternal God, like a master builder,
you have put your Spirit within us,
and have fashioned each of us
into a holy temple.

Upon the foundation of your saving love,
    we follow in the footsteps of Christ,
        offering you our tithes and offerings,
            that the hungry may be fed
                and the naked may be clothed.
May these gifts be signs of our commitment
    to be perfect in our loving,
        even as you are perfect. Amen.

SENDING FORTH

Benediction (Leviticus 19, Matthew 5)
Be perfect in your loving, even as God,
your heavenly Mother and Father, is perfect.
    We will love our neighbor as ourselves.
Be holy in thought, word, and deed,
even as God, the master builder of your life, is holy.
    We will love our enemies,
    and pray for those who persecute us.
Belong to Christ in your living,
even as Christ, the foundation of faith, belongs to God.
    We will rejoice in the Spirit of God
    that dwells within us.

CONTEMPORARY OPTIONS

Gathering Words (Psalm 119, 1 Corinthians 3, Matthew 5)
You belong to God.
    In God, we are holy,
    for God is holy.
You belong to Christ.
    In Christ, we are loving,
    for Christ is loving.
You belong to the Spirit.
    In the Spirit, we are perfect,
    for the Spirit is perfect.
Come! Let us worship the God of love.

Praise Sentences (Leviticus 19, Matthew 5)
Our God is a holy God.
    Praise the One who makes us holy.
Our God is a loving God.
    Praise the One who makes us whole.
Our God is a transforming God.
    Praise the One who perfects us in holy love.

MARCH 2, 2014

Transfiguration Sunday

B. J. Beu

COLOR

White

SCRIPTURE READINGS

Exodus 24:12-18; Psalm 99; 2 Peter 1:16-21;
Matthew 17:1-9

THEME IDEAS

God tells Moses to go up the mountain and wait—wait
for instruction, wait for a taste of God's awesome power,
wait for the next big experience of the holy. As people of
faith, we spend a lot of time waiting. And no matter how
faithfully we wait, it seems that we are never quite ready
when the moment of revelation and mystery occurs. Jesus'
disciples discovered that on the mountaintop when Christ
was transfigured before them. Yes, Transfiguration Sunday is about God's light and power, but it is also about
waiting, and being ready when God's light shines upon
us anew.

INVITATION AND GATHERING

Call to Worship (Exodus 24, Matthew 17)

Climb the mountain of God and wait...
wait for God's glory, which shines like the sun.

**We will climb the mountain of God
and wait for the dawn.**
Climb the mountain of God and wait . . .
wait to see Jesus as he truly is.
**We will climb the mountain of God
and wait for Christ to reveal the heart of God.**
Climb the mountain of God and wait . . .
wait to gain courage for the terror of the night.
**We will climb the mountain of God
and wait for the Spirit to dispel the darkness.**
Climb the mountain of God and wait . . .
wait to behold God's glory.
**We will climb the mountain of God
and wait to see God's light shining like the sun.**

Opening Prayer (Exodus 24, Matthew 17)
Source of Light and Love,
as you appeared to your servant Moses
like a devouring fire on Mount Sinai,
so appear to us in power and might
during our time of worship;
as you revealed to Christ's disciples
the light within their beloved friend and master,
so reveal your light to us
in acts of Christian love and sharing
during our time together.
Transform us with the light of your hope and love,
that our souls might shine your light
through Christ, our Light,
into a world shrouded in darkness
and despair. Amen.

PROCLAMATION AND RESPONSE

Prayer of Confession (Exodus 24, Matthew 17)
Mighty God, we envy Moses and Peter, James and John
for their privileged journey
up your holy mountain.

We imagine ourselves faring better than they,
    as they fell to the ground in terror
        in the presence of your glory.
But we're not so sure.
Would we have the courage of Moses
    to wait a week for your appearance,
        while shrouded in cloud and mist?
Would we have the fortitude
    to endure for forty days
        in the presence of power
            that coursed like a devouring fire?
Test our hearts, O God.
Call us up your mountain,
    that we might face our fears
        and prove ourselves worthy
            of your holy calling. Amen.

Words of Assurance (Matthew 17)
With tenderness and grace, Jesus says to us:
    "Get up and do not be afraid."
In the light of the one who was transfigured
    to show us the power and glory of God,
    we are forgiven and offered strength for the journey.

Introduction to the Word (2 Peter 1)
Be attentive to the word of God, for it is like a lamp shining in a dark place until the day dawns and the morning star rises in our hearts. Listen for the word of God, and you will see the dawn.

Response to the Word (Exodus 24, Psalm 99, 2 Peter 1, Matthew 17)
God speaks from the mountaintop.
God speaks from a pillar of cloud.
God speaks from the skies above.
God speaks from the earth below.
God speaks that we might hear.
God speaks that we might know.
God speaks and is speaking still.

THANKSGIVING AND COMMUNION

Offering Prayer

Light of Light,
  in the midst of our gloom and despair,
    you have blessed us with your radiance
      and your love.
Illumine these gifts,
  that the world may see your light
    shining in today's offering.
Illumine our very lives,
  that our souls may be radiant like Christ
    shining with power upon the mountaintop. Amen.

SENDING FORTH

Benediction (Exodus 24, 2 Peter 1, Matthew 17)

Do not fear to climb the mountain of God.
  We will walk in the light and truth of God.
Do not fear the voice that calls from heaven.
  We will hear the call to follow Jesus.
Do not fear the glory of God
that appears like a devouring fire.
  We will bathe in the wonder of our God.
Do not fear to shine the light of Christ in the world.
  We will be like lamps shining in the dark.
Do not fear, for God goes with us.

CONTEMPORARY OPTIONS

Gathering Words (Psalm 99)

Come worship the Lord.
  Praise the Lord on high.
Worship the Lord from the mountaintop.
  Worship our great and awesome God.
The Lord is king.
  Let the peoples tremble.

Let the earth quake before our God.
Let the nations revere the Lord of life.
Come worship the Lord.
Praise the Lord on high.

Praise Sentences (Psalm 99)
Praise God's great and awesome name.
Praise God's glorious deeds.
The Lord is king!
The Lord is king!
The Lord is king!

MARCH 5, 2014

Ash Wednesday
Hans Holznagel

COLOR

Purple

SCRIPTURE READINGS

Joel 2:1-2, 12-17; Psalm 51:1-17; 2 Corinthians 5:20b–6:10; Matthew 6:1-6, 16-21

THEME IDEAS

The Lenten journey launched by today's readings is modest, quiet, even secret. Through many disciplines, now is the acceptable time to rediscover, with God's help, our honest, secret hearts, confident that God sees in secret. This inward journey may require courage, but it also produces strength to face the world's afflictions with truthful speech, righteousness, and even joy: having nothing and yet possessing everything. The worship resources below are designed for use with a service that includes the imposition of ashes.

INVITATION AND GATHERING

Call to Worship (Psalm 51)
Have mercy on us, O God,
according to your steadfast love,
according to your mercy.

Wash and cleanse us thoroughly, O God,
according to your steadfast love,
   according to your mercy.
You desire inward truth, O God.
   Therefore teach us wisdom
   in the secret places of our hearts,
according to your steadfast love,
   according to your mercy. Amen.

Opening Prayer (Joel 2, Psalm 51, 2 Corinthians 5–6)
We turn our faces toward you
   in a special way today, O God,
      seeking wisdom for the Lenten journey ahead
         and for the paths we walk in life.
Center our spirits this day
   for an inward journey of reconciliation
      to our true selves,
         and thus to you.
In Jesus' name, we pray. Amen.

PROCLAMATION AND RESPONSE

Prayer of Confession (Psalm 51)
The commitment you seek, O God,
   seems out of reach.
We imagine that to properly serve you,
   we must be holy, overtly spiritual,
      and confident in our faith.
In our eyes, we are none of these things.
Remind us, Holy One,
   by the simple touch of ash this day,
      that the journey you have in mind
         is accessible to us all,
            and requires only a desire
               to find the secret heart of truth
                  within ourselves.
Lead on, O God,
   and journey with us, we pray. Amen.

Words of Assurance (Matthew 6, Joel 2, 2 Corinthians 5–6)

Jesus assures us that God especially loves
a humble prayer, a secret prayer.
God is gracious and merciful,
abounding in steadfast love.
Now is the acceptable time.
Be reconciled to God. Amen.

Response to the Word (Matthew 6, Psalm 51, 2 Corinthians 5–6)

God of heart, God of steadfast love,
make our spirits right,
make our witness strong. Amen.

THANKSGIVING AND COMMUNION

Invitation to the Imposition of Ashes (Joel 2, Psalm 51, 2 Corinthians 5–6)

God says: "Return to me with all your hearts, with fasting, with weeping, and with sorrow; tear your hearts and not your clothing. Return . . . , for [God] is merciful and compassionate, very patient, full of faithful love, and ready to forgive." In the forty days ahead, may you search yourself and find truth, may you seek truth and speak it, may you have nothing and yet possess everything. However you observe this season, let the journey start with humble ashes, marking hand, face, and spirit— signifying our commitment and openness to being found anew by God.

Prayer Following the Imposition of Ashes (Psalm 51)

You desire truth in the inward being, O God;
therefore teach me wisdom in my secret heart.
Create in me a clean heart, O God,
and put a new and right spirit within me.
Restore to me the joy of your salvation,
and sustain in me a willing spirit. Amen.

SENDING FORTH

Benediction (Psalm 51, 2 Corinthians 5–6, Matthew 6)
Go forth on your heart's journey,
 strong in the face of afflictions,
 speaking truth,
 and knowing that you are loved well by God.
Go in peace. Amen.

CONTEMPORARY OPTIONS

Gathering Words or Invitation to Imposition of Ashes (Psalm 51)
After a fire, after its warmth and light are gone,
 after its fuel burns away, ash remains.
This simple substance, reminder of flame,
 marks us with hope:
 the hope of warmth and light renewed,
 the hope of barriers consumed.
Let our Lenten journey begin.

Praise Sentences (Psalm 51)
Return to me with all your heart, says our God.
 Now is the time! Now is the day!
Bring your broken heart. Return!
 Now is the time! Now is the day!
Bring your secret heart. Return!
 Now is the time! Now is the day!
 Create in me a clean heart, O God,
 and put a new and right spirit within me. Amen!

MARCH 9, 2014

First Sunday in Lent

B. J. Beu

COLOR

Purple

SCRIPTURE READINGS

Genesis 2:15-17; 3:1-7; Psalm 32; Romans 5:12-19;
Matthew 4:1-11

THEME IDEAS

Today's scriptures highlight the reality of temptation in
human life. Adam and Eve succumbed to temptation
whereas Jesus did not. Whether or not we accept Paul's
suggestion that death entered the human condition
through Adam's transgression, most Christian theology
posits that we now have the power to avoid our own
temptations. To avoid robbing this Sunday of its theological depth, we must take seriously scripture's claim that
Jesus was tempted by the devil in the wilderness. Feeding people is good. Demonstrating God's power to rescue
us is good. Having Jesus rule the world with righteousness would be good. What Jesus would have had to sacrifice for these good outcomes is what made those
temptations wrong. The temptation to choose a lesser
good because it is easier than pursuing a great good is
something we all can relate to.

INVITATION AND GATHERING

Call to Worship (Psalm 32)
Happy are those whose transgression is forgiven.
Happy are those who receive God's mercy.
Rejoice and be glad, you upright in heart.
Shout for joy, you people of God.
Happy are those whose transgression is forgiven.
Happy are those who receive God's mercy.

Opening Prayer (Matthew 4)
Faithful Traveler,
   walk with us
      as we journey with Christ
         through the season of Lent;
   abide with us and strengthen us
      as we face the many temptations
         that befall us each and every day.
Save us from the time of trial,
   and send your angels to strengthen us
      when we consider taking the easy way out.
Be our God, and we will be your people—
   a people raised to newness of life
      through the gift of your Spirit
         and the love of your Son. Amen.

PROCLAMATION AND RESPONSE

Prayer of Confession (Matthew 4)
Holy One, we do not always face temptation well.
We heed the rumblings of our stomachs
   and settle for loaves of bread
      when we are starving for the words of life
         that come from your mouth, O God.
We put you to the test,
   seeking signs of your favor before others
      when we should "be still"
         and know that you are God.

67

We place our trust in deceitful leaders
   who promise us a better and easier life
      when we should be putting our faith
         in you alone.
Forgive us, O God.
In the desert experiences of our lives,
   help us find ways to resist temptation,
      that we might be found worthy of your calling,
         through Jesus Christ, our Lord. Amen.

Words of Assurance (Psalm 32, Romans 5)
When we acknowledge our failings before God,
   God forgives our sin and wipes away our shame.
Receive forgiveness and mercy
   through the free gift of God's grace in Christ.

Passing the Peace of Christ (Romans 5)
Christ's justifying love brings peace to all who embrace the living God. Turn to one another and share the wondrous gift of God's peace in Christ.

Response to the Word (Psalm 32)
God has instructed us and taught us the way we should go. Do not be like horses or mules, dumb beasts without understanding that must be curbed with bit and bridle. Rather, let us freely offer our thanksgiving and prayers to God. Let us rejoice in the One who leads us into life.

THANKSGIVING AND COMMUNION

Offering Prayer (Matthew 4)
Holy One of Israel,
   as we provide loaves of bread
      for those who hunger,
         may we be living bread as well,
            that our offerings may feed the spirit
            as well as the body;
   as we seek to bring justice to our world,
      may we embody faith in your righteous love,

that the world may know
the source of their hope. Amen.

SENDING FORTH

Benediction (Psalm 32, Matthew 4)
Though life is full of temptation,
God will see us through.
We rejoice in the One who strengthens us.
Though life is full of times of trial,
Christ walks with us every step of the way.
We rejoice in the One who shares our journey.
Though life is full of obstacles to faith,
the Spirit eases our burden.
We rejoice in the One who leads us home.
Go with God.

CONTEMPORARY OPTIONS

Gathering Words (Genesis 2, 3; Romans 5)
Forbidden fruit is such a delight to the eye.
God is our delight.
Forbidden pleasures tug at us each day.
God is our joy.
Temptation is everywhere.
We can live as God intends,
through Christ, who strengthens us.
Let us sing to the Lord,
who saves us from the time of trial.
Sing to the Lord, our delight and our joy!

Praise Sentences (Psalm 32)
Be glad in the Lord.
Shout for joy, O people of God.
Sing and dance before the Lord.
Shout for joy, O people of God.
Be glad in the Lord.

MARCH 16, 2014

Second Sunday in Lent
Laura Jaquith Bartlett

COLOR
Purple

SCRIPTURE READINGS
Genesis 12:1-4a; Psalm 121; Romans 4:1-5, 13-17;
John 3:1-17

THEME IDEAS
A crucial aspect of the Lenten journey is the invitation to
make a choice. First, we must choose whether or not to
even participate in this journey. Ash Wednesday gives us
the opportunity to say yes to that choice. But the decisions
don't end there! The Lent 1 readings outline the choices
we are confronted with when temptation knocks on the
door. And the Lent 2 readings present the choice between
blessing and curse. In the very short Genesis passage,
Abram makes the choice look easy, but the psalmist reminds us that we constantly look for blessings in the
wrong places. Even when God's own Son shows us the
way to salvation, like Nicodemus before us, we have trouble choosing to accept the blessing offered. What choice
will we make today?

INVITATION AND GATHERING

Call to Worship (Genesis 12, Psalm 121, John 3)

Come, all who need help!
Our help comes from God,
the one who made heaven and earth.
Come, all who desire blessing!
Our blessing comes from God,
the God of Abraham, the God of the ages.
Come, all who long for salvation!
Our salvation comes from Jesus Christ,
the one sent by God to save the world.

Opening Prayer (Genesis 12, Psalm 121, John 3)

God of the ages,
    we come into this holy space
        asking for your blessing,
            only to find that the abundance of your love
                is already around us.
Open our eyes to see the blessing of your creation
    in the beauty all around us.
Open our ears to hear the blessing of your word
    as it is proclaimed in story and song this day.
Open our hearts to experience the blessing of faith
    through the gentle touch of a friend
        or the supportive smile of a stranger.
And open our doors,
    that we may become vessels of your blessing
        to a world still in need of salvation.
All this we pray in the name of Jesus Christ. Amen.

PROCLAMATION AND RESPONSE

Prayer of Confession (Genesis 12, John 3)

God of salvation,
    you shower our lives and our world with love,
        yet we too often turn away from your blessing.
It is just so easy to complain!
There are little annoyances each day,

but they pile up into a mountainous burden
    that becomes a curse on our lives.
Free us from our unwise choices, O God.
When we are distracted and confused,
    redirect our attention to the abundant opportunities
      to experience your love.
During this Lenten journey, focus our hearts on you,
    that we may choose the blessing of salvation
      offered us each day through Jesus Christ,
        in whom we pray. Amen.

Words of Assurance (Genesis 12, John 3)
God did not send Jesus into the world to condemn it,
    but that the world might be saved through him.
Through the saving love of Jesus Christ,
    you are forgiven and blessed!

Passing the Peace of Christ (Genesis 12)
God's blessings are all around us, in all the families of the earth. As human beings created in God's own image, we carry that divine blessing in our DNA! Knowing that, turn now to one another and offer these words:
    "You are blessed by God, and you are a blessing from God."

Prayer of Preparation or Response to the Word (Genesis 12, John 3)
God of ages past and days to come,
    open our hearts to the message of your love.
Bless us with your truth and wisdom,
    that we might be a blessing to others,
      revealing your promises to the world
        in our words and actions.
Blow through our lives with your Spirit,
    that we may be born anew,
      with love and faith for all to see.
In Christ's name, we pray. Amen.

(Mary J. Scifres)

—OR—

Response to the Word (Genesis 12, Psalm 121, John 3)

The palmist sang of two options when we need help:
Look to the hills alone,
or look to the One who made the hills.
We will look to God!
People of God, the choice is before us:
Curse or blessing?
We choose blessing!
God's only Son has come into the world
to offer a choice: Condemnation or salvation?
We choose the salvation of Jesus Christ!

THANKSGIVING AND COMMUNION

Invitation to the Offering

Through this invitation to share our gifts, we acknowledge that God has blessed us abundantly, and that we are to be a blessing to the world. In the very act of giving, in every act of bestowing blessings on another, we find that we are blessed yet again. I encourage you now to enter fully into this amazing cycle of blessing.

Offering Prayer (Genesis 12, John 3)

Generous God,
    you shower us with gifts,
        including the greatest gift of all,
            your own Son, Jesus Christ.
In thanksgiving and praise,
    we offer you our time, our money,
        our very selves.
In these actions,
    we proclaim our intention to be a blessing
        in your world. Amen.

SENDING FORTH

Benediction (Psalm 121, John 3)

As you leave this place,
    lift up your eyes to the Lord!

The One who sent Jesus Christ,
    as salvation for all the world,
    will never desert you.
The Lord will keep your going out and your coming in,
    from this time on, and forevermore.
Go now in peace, with God's blessing.

CONTEMPORARY OPTIONS

Gathering Words (Genesis 12, Psalm 121)

Look up to the mountains;
does our strength come from mountains?
    No, our strength comes from God,
    who made heaven and earth and mountains.
Look to the world for affirmation of our worth;
does our blessing come from the world?
    No, our blessing comes from God,
    who has blessed all the families of the earth.

—OR—

Gathering Words (John 3)

Listen, the wind is blowing where it will.
    Blow, Holy Spirit, with wisdom and truth.
Listen, God is speaking still.
    Blow, Holy Spirit, with wisdom and truth.
Listen, God's Spirit is in this place.
    Blow, Holy Spirit, with wisdom and truth.

(Mary J. Scifres)

Praise Sentences (John 3)

God loved the world so much!
    God gave the world Jesus, God's only Son.
God loved the world so much!
    God gave the world eternal life.
God loved the world so much!
    God gave the world salvation
    through Jesus Christ.

MARCH 23, 2014

Third Sunday in Lent
Mary J. Scifres

COLOR
Purple

SCRIPTURE READINGS
Exodus 17:1-7; Psalm 95; Romans 5:1-11; John 4:5-42

THEME IDEAS
The waters of faith spring forth in all of today's readings, but most profoundly in Jesus' encounter with the Samaritan woman in John 4. Whereas the quarreling and grumbling Israelites rejected God's gift even after Moses miraculously quenched their thirst with water from a rock, the Samaritan woman immediately accepted Jesus' offer of living water. Her faith led to some of Jesus' most profound words in all the Gospels, and dozens of sermons can be crafted from their dialogue. But for today, I am most inspired by the woman's faith and the living water that is ours when we walk in faith with Christ.

INVITATION AND GATHERING

Call to Worship (John 4)
Drink the living waters...
the living waters of faith in Christ.
Taste the bread of life...
the grace and love of God.

Come to the well of wisdom . . .
where thirst for righteousness is quenched.
Come, let us worship in spirit and truth.

Opening Prayer

Living water,
flow through our worship this day.
Quench our thirst for your wisdom and truth,
that we may grow in faith and love.
Fill us with streams of your Spirit,
that we may know you more fully. Amen.

PROCLAMATION AND RESPONSE

Call to Confession (John 4)

Jesus asks a Samaritan woman of divorce and disrepute
to give him a drink of water. In return, Jesus offers her waters of eternal life. Like her, we too are invited to drink of
Christ's grace and talk with our God—no matter our history, no matter our shortcomings. Come to the living
water. Christ will hear our prayer.

Prayer of Confession (John 4)

Gracious God,
grant us the water of your grace.
Flow through our sins and our sorrows
with your mercy and your love.
Forgive us, restore us, renew us, and reclaim us.
Spring forth in us,
that we may move forward in faith,
forgiven and free,
to follow your path
and proclaim your love.

Words of Assurance (John 4)

Come and see!
Christ knows our actions and forgives us still.
We are forgiven and made new in Christ!

Introduction to the Word (John 4)

Come and see the presence of Christ in the word of God.
Come and hear the stories of faith that invite us to believe
and be transformed. Listen for the word of God.

Response to the Word (John 4)

Eternal God, gush up in our lives
  like a spring of living water.
Give us the faith of a child,
    that we may invite others
      to "come and see!"
      your presence in their lives.
Give us the confidence of the Samaritan woman,
    that we may share the good news of your love
      with all we meet. Amen.

THANKSGIVING AND COMMUNION

Offering Prayer (John 4)

Pour out your Spirit on these gifts.
May they spring forth as living waters—
    waters of life, grace, and hope
      for a world in need.

Invitation to Communion (John 4)

Come and see.
  All things are ready.
Drink of the wine.
  This is the living water of Christ,
  love for all to share.
Taste of the bread.
  This is the bread of life,
  the presence of Christ within.
Come to the table, where all are welcome.
  We come to the table of love.

SENDING FORTH

Benediction (John 4)

With excitement and joy,
go forth to proclaim God's love.
  God has done great things for us!

11

With hope and faith,
go forth to share the water of life.
Christ has done great things for us,
offering love to share with all!

CONTEMPORARY OPTIONS

Gathering Words (John 4)

Are you alone at noon,
drawing water from a well that never satisfies?
Come and see the love of God!
Are you pursuing hopeless relationships
and dead end paths?
Come and see the love of God!
Are you wondering which god is real,
which religion is right?
Come and see the love of God!
Are you yearning for hope, wishing for faith,
wanting to believe again?
Come and see the love of God!
Come and see, for God sees you.
Come and hear, for God is listening.
Come and seek, for Christ is here.
Christ will find us
and offer us the waters of life and love!

Praise Sentences (John 4)

Come and see!
Christ is here! God is living with us!
Come and see!
Christ is here! God is living with us!

MARCH 30, 2014

Fourth Sunday in Lent
One Great Hour of Sharing
Sharon McCart

COLOR

Purple

SCRIPTURE READINGS

1 Samuel 16:1-13; Psalm 23; Ephesians 5:8-14; John 9:1-41

THEME IDEAS

When we see clearly, our lives are transformed. But seeing God clearly, recognizing Christ, and perceiving the anointing of God requires the work and light of the Holy Spirit. When we have the light of the Spirit, we see God and understand things more fully, we see others with the eyes of Christ. God does not value us for what we look like. God sees into our hearts and knows what we feel and believe. Anyone can be called by God to achieve greatness. And everyone is cared for by the Good Shepherd, who gives us all that we need. For we are all "children of light," created by the One who is light, and in whom there is no darkness at all. Yet, we are also all blind and in need of healing so that we might be the sight of God, clear and undistorted by our sin, our hurts, our agendas, and our prejudices. The light of the world shines, and the darkness that is in the world has not overcome it—not in our individual lives, not in our collective lives, not in the history of the world as a whole. The light will not be extinguished. We must let it shine through us!

INVITATION AND GATHERING

Call to Worship (Ephesians 5, John 9)
When the world is dark and full of hate and fear,
when we cannot see God
we will turn on the light.
When we cannot find our way back to love and peace
we will turn on the light.
When our vision dims due to the darkness within
we will turn on the light.
Christ opens our eyes with the gift of sight.
The light of the world is Jesus Christ.
Come and worship the one
who brings sight to the blind.
Hallelujah! Praise God, the light of the world!

Opening Prayer (Ephesians 5, John 9)
Gracious God, who created us in God's own image,
we are grateful for all that you have done for us,
for all that you are doing in us,
and for all that you will do through us.
Open our eyes to see your presence among us,
moving in powerful ways at all times
and in all places.
Open our ears to hear familiar words in new ways—
ways that will change us and challenge us
to become the people you created us to be.
Grant us the power and the courage
to come out of the darkness
and into the light of Jesus Christ,
that we may serve you by serving others.
We love you with all our heart, soul, mind,
and strength. Amen.

PROCLAMATION AND RESPONSE

Prayer of Confession (1 Samuel 16, Ephesians 5, John 9)

Forgiving God, in a world filled with so much pain,
we would rather shut our eyes and be blind
than see things as they really are.
Grant us the courage to face the reality of our world,
and give us the strength to bring your light
to those who walk in darkness.
Help us see others as you see them,
and forgive us when we do not trust you enough
to open our eyes to the possibilities before us.
Heal our self-inflicted blindness, O God,
and lead us in the footsteps
of the Light of the World,
who reveals your glory in his life,
his teachings, and his love.
In his holy name, we pray. Amen.

Words of Assurance (Psalm 23)

Christ came to lead us in paths of righteousness
and to guide us through our lives.
Christ is with us in times of danger and times of peace.
The goodness and mercy of God
are given to us each and every day of our lives.
God forgives us for our failings, upholds us in love,
and leads us to the place
that Christ has prepared for us.
Believe in your heart that God loves you
and forgives you.
We believe! God help our unbelief!

Response to the Word (Ephesians 5, John 9)

In the light of God, all is made clear. We see how much
God loves us and how much God loves all people. We see
Christ, the Light of the World, in Scripture and in our
lives; and although we once were blind, now we see!

THANKSGIVING AND COMMUNION

Offering Prayer (Psalm 23)
God of light and love and peace,
    we praise your name
        for leading us in paths of righteousness,
            that we may come into your presence,
            forgiven and free.
We give you thanks for guiding us to this place:
    where we may rest beside the still waters
        of your grace,
    where we are filled with the good gifts
        of your goodness and mercy.
We worship you with all that we are,
    and we bless your name for all that we will be
        as we continue on our journey—
            a journey that leads us to your kingdom,
                where we will dwell with you forever.
We offer you these gifts,
    that you might bless them and send them out
        into the valley of the shadow of death,
            and everywhere in need of your light. Amen.

SENDING FORTH

Benediction (Psalm 23, Ephesians 5)
Go into the world, carrying the light of Christ
into the darkness!
We go, with hearts full and eyes open!
Receive God's love and care,
and share that love and care with others!
We go, with eyes reflecting God's light
and hands open to share it!
May you walk in the light of Christ
all the days of your life!
We will follow Christ wherever he leads us! Amen!

CONTEMPORARY OPTIONS

Gathering Words (Psalm 23)

Let's go to some place green and cool!
>**But we have to go through that industrial area
>to get there!**

We'll just take the shortcut by the river.
>**And let's take something to eat!**

Good idea! We can share it with the people
over on the other side!
>**They never have enough to eat!**

And tonight we can sleep out under the stars!
>**We are part of God's creation
>and God will take care of us!**

God is good, all the time!
>**And all the time, God is good!**

—OR—

Gathering Words

Wake up, sleepy heads.
>**It's too early. Can't you turn the lights down?**

Christ's light is shining. It's time to wake up.
>**A few more minutes would be great.**
>**Does it have to be this bright?**

Christ is the light of the world.
>**Does that make us children of the light?**

You know it does. Now wake up!
Worship the Lord of light.
>**We worship the Light of the world!**

(B. J. Beu)

Praise Sentences (Psalm 23)

God gives us what we need!
>**God shows us how to live!**

Praise God for being with us no matter what!
>**Love the Lord your God,
>with all your heart, soul, mind, and strength!**

APRIL 6, 2014

Fifth Sunday in Lent
John Indermark

COLOR
Purple

SCRIPTURE READINGS
Ezekiel 37:1-14; Psalm 130; Romans 8:6-11; John 11:1-45

THEME IDEAS
Hope is not only a life and death matter, hope is a life *in* death matter. Hope finds its greatest challenge, and shines its greatest light, when life stands in the face of death and affirms that God remains trustworthy. Ezekiel is called to prophesy such hope in a valley of dried bones and lost dreams. The psalmist proclaims hope from the depths, as one who waits for the gift of a morning yet to dawn. And Jesus, stricken with a grief born of love, speaks hope into Lazarus's tomb, calling his friend forth as a sign of God's glory and of our hope.

INVITATION AND GATHERING

Call to Worship (Ezekiel 37, John 11)
Coming from places that have seen better days,
God bids us to celebrate this day,
a day full of new possibilities.

Coming with our breath taken away by grief,
the Holy Spirit breathes new life within us,
renewing our connection with God
and with one another.
Coming to worship seeking a hope that will endure,
Christ unbinds the fetters that hold us in death,
speaking in word and sacrament,
and building community for holy service.

Opening Prayer (Psalm 130, John 11)
God of life, present and promised,
you are the One to whom we call:
for you are the One who hears,
and you are the One who acts,
bringing us new life
with your grace and love and power.
Lead us in our time of worship,
that we may be prepared to follow your lead
in places where life is at risk—
places where hope seems far away,
places where dreams die during sleep.
When we leave these walls,
help us live the teachings we proclaim
within this place of worship,
through Jesus Christ our Lord. Amen.

PROCLAMATION AND RESPONSE

Prayer of Confession (Ezekiel 37, Psalm 130, John 11)
Forgive us, O God,
when we see the world
through rose-colored glasses
rather than as it really is,
much less the way you seek it to be.
Forgive us, Holy One,
when we forsake lively and risky faith
calling us to be agents of change in our world
for the bland conviction that all will be well.

86

Renew us with your grace
    and ground us with your Spirit,
        that we might be empowered to live,
            in word and deed,
                as testimonies to the power
                    of your love over the grave.
In Jesus Christ, we pray. Amen.

Words of Assurance (Ezekiel 37, Romans 8)
The God we serve is the God of life,
    the God of hope, the God of new beginnings—
    even for dried-up bones and shattered dreams.
That rattling of bones in Ezekiel's vision
    may be heard as the shackles that once held us down
    in fear, sin, prejudice, and guilt.
God defies these deadly entanglements
    with the power of life.
This we trust, and by this we live.
Thanks be to God!

Response to the Word (Ezekiel 37, John 11)
In the midst of a valley filled with bones, amidst the
stench of a tomb's death and decay, a voice cries out in
the name of life. And in holy mystery, life comes forth.
These are the stories we are told. But are these the stories
we will trust? Are these the stories we will live by?

THANKSGIVING AND COMMUNION

Offering Prayer (Ezekiel 37, John 11)
From your hands, O God,
    come the blessings that make life possible,
        even the very gift of life itself.
In gratitude and thanks,
    receive from our hands this portion of our labors.
By your Spirit's leading,
    may we use these gifts to bless the life of others
        with the assurance of love,
            the promise of hope,
                and the course of justice.

This we do to your glory. Amen.

Invitation to Communion (Ezekiel 37)

Ezekiel prophesied life to broken and scattered bones.
    Jesus offered the bread of life
    to soon-to-be-scattered disciples.
In a field where life had been poured out,
Ezekiel promised the outpouring of God's Spirit.
    At this table, in a cup poured out,
    and in bread broken, Jesus promises
    new life in God's kingdom.
Let us gather at God's table, and remember.
Let us gather at God's table, and hope.

SENDING FORTH

Benediction (Psalm 130, Romans 8)

We are a people loved by God.
    We will live as signs of this love.
We are a people blessed with hope.
    We will live in light of this hope.
May the love of God, the grace of Christ,
and the courage of the Spirit, strengthen our faith
and set us loose to share God's love with all.
    Amen and amen!

CONTEMPORARY OPTIONS

Gathering Words (Ezekiel 37, John 11)

God says: I will put my Spirit within you,
and you shall live. Will you believe?
    Lord, we lift your name on high.
    Lord, we love to sing your praises.
Jesus says: I am the resurrection and the life.
Will you live as if this were so?
    Lord, we lift your name on high.
    Lord, we love to sing your praises.
Jesus called: Lazarus, come forth!
Jesus still calls: *(name of congregation)*, come forth!

Lord, we lift your name on high.
Lord, we love to sing your praises.

Praise Sentences (Psalm 130)
Hope in God, whose love is steadfast,
whose power redeems.
Hope in God, whose love is steadfast,
whose power redeems.

APRIL 13, 2014

Palm/Passion Sunday
Leigh Anne Taylor

COLOR
Purple

PALM SUNDAY READINGS
Matthew 21:1-11; Psalm 118:1-2, 19-29

PASSION SUNDAY READINGS
Isaiah 50:4-9a; Psalm 31:9-16; Philippians 2:5-11; Matthew 26:14–27:66 (27:11-54)

THEME IDEAS
The readings for Palm/Passion Sunday provide the narrative of Jesus' final week—beginning with the story of his triumphant entry into Jerusalem, to the story of his final Passover meal with the disciples, and ending with the story of his betrayal, arrest, trial, beating, and crucifixion. Psalm 118 is a pilgrim's song for Jesus' triumphant entry into Jerusalem: Hosanna! "Blessed is the one who comes in the name of the LORD!" Psalm 31 and Isaiah 50 speak words that Christ himself might have uttered as he suffered; and our reading from Philippians is an ancient hymn proclaiming the Lordship of Christ.

INVITATION AND GATHERING

Call to Worship (Matthew 21, Psalm 118)
Come into God's house with thanksgiving and praise.
We come in the name of Jesus, God's Son.
Come into God's house with worship and prayer.
Where would we be without your love, O God?
With all that we have, and with all that we are,
we praise your holy name, Lord.
Blessed are you who come in the name of the Lord.
Blessed are you who gather in Christ's name.
Bring yourselves before him, all you who love him.
See how humble he is? He will receive you.
Save us, Jesus; save us now!
Hosanna to the son of David!

—*OR*—

Call to Worship (Psalm 118)
This is the day that the Lord has made.
Let us rejoice and be glad in it.
Blessed is the one who comes in the name of the Lord.
God's steadfast love endures forever.
The stone that the builders rejected
has become the chief cornerstone.
This is the Lord's doing.
It is marvelous in our eyes.
Bind the festival procession with branches.
Jesus is the gate of the Lord.
The righteous enter through him.
This is the day that the Lord has made.
Let us rejoice and be glad in it.

(*B. J. Beu*)

Opening Prayer (Matthew 21, 26, Psalm 118)
Holy Jesus, on this day when you were welcomed as king,
we remember that in one week's time
you were scorned and reviled
by the same people who greeted you
with shouts of praise and adoration;

91

on this day when you were greeted with hosannas,
    we remember that your closest followers
        denied that they knew you,
           and abandoned you
                as you faced the cross.
We are astonished at the complete and utter failure
    of human love.
In the light of our failure, we are even more astonished
    that through you, God's love for all humanity
        is made manifest.
We have nowhere to dwell but in your love. Amen.

PROCLAMATION AND RESPONSE

Prayer of Confession (Matthew 26, Psalm 31)
Lord, when reading the story of your passion and death,
    it is easy to criticize the actions of people
        who turned their backs on you,
        who betrayed you,
        who mocked you,
           and who murdered you;
    it is harder for us to see ourselves reflected
      in the worst of human behavior.
Forgive us when we'd rather blame others
    than take responsibility for ourselves.
Help us see in our own lives:
    where we have failed to stay close to you in prayer,
    where we have denied you,
    where we have betrayed you,
    where we have stood by silent
        while others mocked or hated another.
Forgive us, Lord,
    and have mercy on us.
Save us in your steadfast love. Amen.

Words of Assurance (Psalm 118)
Give thanks to the Lord, for God is good.
God's steadfast love endures forever.

Let all God's people say:
   God's steadfast love endures forever.
Let us thank the Lord, who has answered us
and has become our salvation.
   Thanks be to God.

Passing the Peace of Christ (Philippians 2)
The great hymn in Philippians looks forward to the day
when "every knee will bow and every tongue confess that
Jesus Christ is Lord." Let us offer one another peace in the
name of Jesus Christ, the Lord.

Introduction to the Word or Prayer of Preparation (Isaiah 50)
Lord God, awaken our ears to listen,
   as those who are eager to hear.
Open our ears and help us hear the story
   of your passion and death,
      as if we were hearing it
         for the very first time. Amen.

Response to the Word (Philippians 2)
From the United Methodist Hymnal: *"Canticle of Christ's Obedience" (#167) and "At the Name of Jesus" (#168).*

THANKSGIVING AND COMMUNION

Invitation to the Offering (Philippians 2)
The depth of Christ's love and the enormity of Christ's offering for us invite us to offer our gifts and our lives as
an endless song of gratitude. Let us offer our gifts with
gladness.

Offering Prayer (Philippians 2)
Holy God, as we offer our gifts and our very selves to you,
   receive this offering as the first measure
      of our gratitude for all that you are
         and all that you have done for us,
            through your Son, Jesus Christ.
Help us continue to sing a song of gratitude

each and every day of our lives,
in the name of Jesus Christ. Amen.

SENDING FORTH

Benediction (Matthew 26)
Pilate washed his hands of him.
Peter denied that he ever knew him.
All the disciples deserted him.
Judas ended his own life after betraying him.
Joseph of Arimathea provided a grave for him.
Mary and the woman stood watch over him.
The centurion proclaimed him to be the Son of God.
The soldiers secured his grave with a stone.
Jesus said to his disciples,
    "I will go ahead of you to Galilee."
Let us go forth into this Holy Week knowing
    that no matter who we are, or what we have done,
    Jesus Christ goes ahead of us to prepare the way.

Benediction (Psalm 118)
The gates of righteousness are thrown wide.
Christ has blessed us with life.
The path of salvation is made plain.
Christ has blessed us with truth.
The cornerstone of our faith is sure.
Christ has blessed us with grace.
The gates of righteousness are thrown wide.

(B. J. Beu)

CONTEMPORARY OPTIONS

Gathering Words (Matthew 21, Psalm 118)
Welcome to this house,
where God's people gather to worship.
We come in the name of Jesus, God's Son.

Praise Sentences (Psalm 118)
Come into God's house with worship and praise.

Where would we be without your love, O God?
Without you, we are nothing.
With all that we have, and all that we are,
we praise you, we bless you,
we worship you, Lord.

APRIL 17, 2014

Holy Thursday
Karin Ellis

COLOR
Purple

SCRIPTURE READINGS
Exodus 12:1-4, (5-10), 11-14; Psalm 116:1-4, 12-19;
1 Corinthians 11:23-26; John 13:1-17, 31b-35

THEME IDEAS
On this holy night, we remember, celebrate, and give thanks to God. The psalmist invites us to worship with thanksgiving and praise. Exodus recounts the story of the Passover, and in the readings from 1 Corinthians and the Gospel of John, we find the story of Jesus' Last Supper with his friends. Common themes run throughout these stories. The Israelites make sacrifices on behalf of God, and Jesus foreshadows the sacrifice he will make on behalf of humanity. The Israelites receive a new beginning as they are led from slavery to freedom, and a new covenant based on unconditional love is established between God and all people through the death and resurrection of Christ. Jesus, the servant, serves his friends, and invites them to become servants of one another. These scriptures invite acts of remembrance and celebration—to give thanks for God's abundant providence, abiding presence, and unconditional love.

INVITATION AND GATHERING

Call to Worship (1 Corinthians 11, John 13)
We have gathered in the dark of night
to remember and give thanks.
We have gathered around the Lord's table
to hear stories of our faith,
to feast on the Word made flesh,
and to proclaim God's abundant love!

—*OR*—

Call to Worship (Psalm 116)
Snares of death surround us.
Call on the name of the Lord and be saved.
The Lord is the cup of our salvation!
Pangs of suffering and grief enfold us.
Call on the name of the Lord and be saved.
The Lord is the cup of our salvation!
Bonds of distress and anguish bind us.
Call on the name of the Lord and be saved.
The Lord is the cup of our salvation!

(B. J. Beu)

Opening Prayer (Psalm 116)
Gracious God,
we have been called here
by your inviting Spirit.
As we come to worship you
and praise your name, we wonder:
"What can we bring you?"
In the dark of the night,
and in the depths of our hearts, we hear your reply:
"Your love is all I require."
So, in thanksgiving and praise,
we bring you our whole selves,
with hearts full to bursting.
Incline our ears to your word,
and open our hearts
to the mystery of this holy night. Amen.

PROCLAMATION AND RESPONSE

Prayer of Confession (Exodus 12, John 13)

Holy Lord,
> on this night, we are like the disciples who asked,
>> "Lord, are you going to wash my feet?"

It is hard to witness acts of selfless service,
> for our actions are rarely so pure.

Forgive our selfish tendencies.
Forgive us when we fail to listen to you
> and live by your example.

Help us listen for your guidance,
> and overcome our shortcomings,
>> that we may become your faithful servants. Amen.

Words of Assurance (John 13)

Brothers and sisters, hear these words of Christ:
> "Just as I have loved you,
> you also should love one another."

We are loved and forgiven and free,
> to once again share God's grace with one another.

Thanks be to God!

Passing the Peace of Christ (Exodus 12)

As families and friends, we are invited to celebrate God's presence with one another. Let us greet one another with the peace and spirit of Christ!

Introduction to the Word (1 Corinthians 11)

May the words of my mouth,
> **and the reflections of our hearts,**

be received with grace,
> **and celebrated with joy.**

Response to the Word (1 Corinthians 11, John 13)

Holy One, we give thanks for your word,
> spoken among us this day.

Help us remember that through brokenness
> comes healing and new life,
>> and through the waters of grace

comes cleansing and rebirth.
May these words be written upon our hearts
and shared with the world,
so all might come to know
your love and grace. Amen.

THANKSGIVING AND COMMUNION

Invitation to the Offering (Psalm 116)

We have been called by God to offer our prayers, our presence, our hearts, and our gifts. In response to God's generous love, let us offer what we can in order to show our thanksgiving and praise.

Offering Prayer (Exodus 12)

Loving God, we give you thanks and praise
for the gifts you have given us.
May these gifts be used to spread your love and grace:
to those who are in exile,
to those who are hurting,
and to all who are in need of your touch.
May these gifts be a celebration
of your presence in our lives! Amen.

Call to Communion (1 Corinthians 11, John 13)

As often as we gather,
we gather in remembrance of Christ.
When we care for another in need,
we care for Christ our Lord.
When we break the bread and share the cup,
we participate in the kingdom of God.
Come, all things are ready.

(Mary J. Scifres)

Communion Prayer (1 Corinthians 11, John 13)

Servant God,
we remember this night
your many gifts of grace and servanthood
as you walked upon this earth;

99

we remember this night
 your many gifts of grace and servanthood
  as you touch our lives today.
With humility and gratitude,
 we come to the table
  and accept your gracious gifts
   of forgiveness and love.

Christ Jesus,
 we remember that night
  when you took a loaf of bread,
  gave thanks, and broke it, saying,
   "This is my body that is for you.
   Do this in remembrance of me."
We remember that in the same way,
 you took the cup and said,
   "This cup is the new covenant of my lifeblood.
   Do this, as often as you drink it,
   in remembrance of me."
We remember on this night
 why we eat this bread and drink this cup:
 to proclaim the great mystery of faith:
 Christ has died. Christ is risen.
 Christ will come again.
Pour out your Holy Spirit on all those gathered here,
 that we might be disciples of your new covenant
  of love and grace.
Pour out your Holy Spirit
 on these gifts of bread and wine,
  that they may be for us
   the life and love of Christ,
  that we may be for the world
   the body of Christ,
    redeemed by your gracious love.

By your Spirit, make us one with Christ,
 one with each other,

and one in ministry to all the world.
In Christ's name we pray. Amen.

(Mary J. Scifres)

SENDING FORTH

Benediction (John 13)

Brothers and sisters, remember this night.
Remember the broken bread, the shared cup,
and the cleansing water.
Go into this night remembering and celebrating
Christ's presence among us.
Go in peace! Amen.

CONTEMPORARY OPTIONS

Gathering Words (Psalm 116, John 13)

In the dark of the evening, guided by candlelight,
we come to remember and to give thanks.
In the solemness of this hour, guided by prayer,
we come to worship, to be fed by God's Spirit,
to be filled with Christ's amazing love!

Praise Sentences (Psalm 116, John 13)

Jesus said, "Just as I have loved you, love one another."
My friends, be filled with the love of Christ!
The love of Christ flows through us
and around us. Praise the Lord!

APRIL 18, 2014

Good Friday: A Service of Tenebrae

B. J. Beu

COLOR

Black or None

SCRIPTURE READINGS

Isaiah 52:13–53:12; Psalm 22; Hebrews 10:16-25;
John 18:1–19:42

TENEBRAE READINGS

Although a traditional Service of Tenebrae contains sixteen readings taken from John 18:1–19:42, this service contains fourteen readings culled from all four Gospels. Just as no Christmas Eve nativity would be complete without the arrival of the magi, no passion account is complete without elements omitted from John's narrative. The readings conclude at Jesus' death, the climax of the passion narrative, and omit the two burial readings (John 19:31-37 and John 19:38-42), which may be included if you wish.

THEME IDEAS

Suffering, rejection, and loss focus our readings. Although Isaiah 52 begins with the exaltation of God's servant, it is a chilling reminder of how easily we turn on God's chosen ones. A Service of Tenebrae, or "darkness," is an extended meditation of Christ's passion. Psalm 22, which Jesus quotes while hanging on the cross, conveys the sense of being abandoned by God when the forces of destruction hold sway. Peter's betrayal of his friend and teacher in the courtyard depicts how low we can sink, despite our love and convictions. *(Note: If your congregation has a gold or brass cross on its Lord's Table, substitute a rough-hewn wooden cross with horseshoe nails at the place of Jesus' hands and feet.)*

INVITATION AND GATHERING

Call to Worship
Were you there when they crucified my Lord?
**We were the hollow echo
of hosannas once spoken in love.**
Were you in the garden when the disciples fell asleep?
We were the betrayal in Judas's kiss.
Were you in the courtyard when the cock crowed?
We were the denial in Peter's mouth.
Were you among the scoffers when Jesus was flogged?
We were the whip in the soldier's hand.
Were you in Pilate's chamber when he washed his hands of Jesus' fate?
**We were the hatred of the crowd,
the indifference in Pilate's heart.**
Were you there when the soldiers dressed Jesus as a king?
We were the mockery in the crown of thorns.
Were you among the spectators at Golgatha?
We were the nails that pierced Jesus' hands and feet.
Were you there when they crucified my Lord?
We were the silence when no bird sang.

Opening Song
"Were You There" (vv. 1-3)

Opening Prayer (Isaiah 52–53, Psalm 22:1 NRSV)
Elusive One, where do you go
when all hope fades,
when we cry out with the psalmist,
"My God, my God,
why have you forsaken me?"

In the midst of our pain and despair,
  we strain to see you
    charging to our rescue.
Yet, in our disbelief and dismay,
  we face the emptiness
    of your absence.
Your ways are beyond us, Holy One,
  shrouding us in mystery.
Be with us in our hour of greatest need,
  and do not abandon us
    when we deny you.

PROCLAMATION AND RESPONSE

First Reading (Luke 22:39-53)
  (The first candle is extinguished.)

Second Reading (John 18:12-14)
  (The second candle is extinguished.)

Song
  "Go to Dark Gethsemane" (vv. 1-2)

Third Reading (Luke 22:54b-62)
  (The third candle is extinguished.)

Litany (John 18)
  There is no warmth in the fire.
    Our blood runs cold as the night.
  The one we love is in peril.
    Our courage blows away like the wind.
  Strangers recognize our fellowship with Jesus.
    Our denial pierces the soul
    like the cock's crow pierces the dawn.
  There is no warmth in the fire.
    Our tears flow cold as the night.

Fourth Reading (John 18:19-23)
  (The fourth candle is extinguished.)

Fifth Reading (Matthew 27:1-2)
(The fifth candle is extinguished.)

Song
"When Jesus Wept" *(done in Taizé style)*

Sixth Reading (Matthew 27:3-10)
(The sixth candle is extinguished.)

Litany (Matthew 27)
Jesus stands condemned.
> **Stop this madness.**

It is too late.
> **We repent of our sin.**

You have been well paid.
> **We don't want your blood money.**

It is yours all the same.
> **Stop this madness.**

It is too late.

Seventh Reading (John 18:33-38)
(The seventh candle is extinguished.)

Song
"What Wondrous Love Is This"

Eighth Reading (Matthew 27:15-24)
(The eighth candle is extinguished.)

Prayer of Confession (Matthew 27)
Holy Mystery,
> it is easier to wash our hands of responsibility
> > than it is to stand up for what we believe;
> it is easier to defer to the judgments of others
> > than it is to take a principled stand.

When we take the easy way out,
> forgive us, O God.

Fill us with the courage of your Son,
> that we may cast off our darkness
> > and embrace your glorious light.

Ninth Reading (Matthew 27:26-31)
(The ninth candle is extinguished.)

Song
"O Sacred Head Now Wounded"

Tenth Reading (Matthew 27:32-37; John 19:20b-21)
(The tenth candle is extinguished.)

Eleventh Reading (Luke 23:35, 39-43)
(The eleventh candle is extinguished.)

Song
"Jesus, Remember Me" *(done in Taizé style)*

Litany
Come to the cross and feel the weight of the world.
   We bring the weight of our sins.
Come to the cross and feel the weight of the world.
   We bring the weight of our desertions and betrayals.
Come to the cross and feel the weight of the world.
   We bring the weight of our accusations and scorn.
Come to the cross and feel the weight of the world.
   We bring the weight of our lives.

Twelfth Reading (Mark 15:33-34)
(The twelfth candle is extinguished.)

Thirteenth Reading (Mark 15:35-36)
(The thirteenth candle is extinguished.)

Fourteenth Reading (Matthew 27:50-51)
(As the description of the earthquake is read, a loud noise is made by a cymbal or other such instrument; then the fourteenth candle is extinguished.)

SENDING FORTH

(Drape the cross with black cloth and extinguish the Christ candle. Have rubrics in the program for the people to depart in silence.)

APRIL 20, 2014

Easter Sunday
Laura Jaquith Bartlett

COLOR
White

SCRIPTURE READINGS
Acts 10:34-43; Psalm 118:1-2, 14-24; Colossians 3:1-4; John
20:1-18 (or Matthew 28:1-10)

THEME IDEAS
How often do we really open our eyes to see the Risen
Christ in our midst? Mary and the disciples saw only
signs that Jesus had been taken away; they were not expecting to encounter a living savior, and so they missed
the clues. How many folks come to church expecting to
encounter a living savior? How many worship leaders
live with that expectation? Maybe this Easter will be an
opportunity to establish the belief in our congregations
that the resurrected Christ *is* in our midst—this week and
every week!

INVITATION AND GATHERING

Call to Worship (Psalm 118, John 20)
Christ is risen!
  God's steadfast love endures forever.
Death never gets the final word.

(alternate line)
[Death has lost its sting.]
God's steadfast love endures forever.
Rejoice in this day of salvation.
God's steadfast love endures forever. Alleluia!

Opening Prayer (Psalm 118, John 20)
Living God,
> rejoicing in this day of resurrection,
> > we have come to celebrate
> > the strength of your love—
> > > a love that triumphs even over death.
As we exult in the miracle of your incarnate love,
> we thank you for the opportunity
> > to encounter the Risen Christ
> here in our midst. Amen.

PROCLAMATION AND RESPONSE

Prayer of Confession (John 20)
Merciful God, we don't always recognize Christ,
> even when we are looking directly
> > at your Incarnate Love.
We cling to our assumptions
> about how life on earth should unfold,
> > forgetting that life in your realm
> > shatters those expectations.
Forgive us when we go through our daily routine,
> forgetting to look for the Risen One.
Forgive us when coming to worship
> is more about seeing our friends
> > than it is about encountering you
> > and our Resurrected Lord.
Open our eyes and our hearts, O God,
> to the full awareness of your presence with us,
> > in each and every moment of our lives.
We pray in the name of the Christ who is alive!
Alleluia and amen.

Words of Assurance (Acts 10)

The testimony of all the prophets is united
in this message of good news:
Everyone who believes in Jesus Christ
receives forgiveness of sins through his name.
Rejoice, for your sins are already forgiven!

Passing the Peace of Christ

I invite you to exchange signs of peace with one another
using these traditional words that have been spoken by
Easter Christians throughout the centuries:
Christ is risen!
Christ is risen indeed! Alleluia!

Prayer of Preparation (John 20)

*(This prayer can be offered by the liturgist or the preacher, or it
could be printed as a unison prayer.)*
Open our ears to hear your Word
proclaimed in this place.
Open our hearts to know your Love
offered in this congregation.
Open our eyes to see your Presence
blessing us in this moment.

Response to the Word (John 20)

*(This response is designed to be presented by two alternating
readers, with the bold print done by both readers.)*
The stone was gone,
so Mary assumed that Christ had been taken away.
The tomb was empty,
so Peter assumed that Christ had been taken away.
The angels had come,
so Mary assumed that Christ had been taken away.
The linens were discarded,
so Peter assumed that Christ had been taken away.
And yet ... [pause]
Christ was risen.
Christ was alive.
Christ was in their midst.
They saw the Living Christ.

When our lives seem empty,
we assume that Christ has been taken away.
When our lives are full of pain,
we assume that Christ has been taken away.
And yet ... *[pause]*
Christ is risen!
Christ is alive!
Christ is in our midst!
Let us open our eyes to see the Living Christ
here with us today!

THANKSGIVING AND COMMUNION

Offering Prayer (Psalm 118, John 20)
Thank you, God,
for the gift of this amazing day of resurrection!
Our hearts are overflowing
with the joy and excitement of Easter.
We pray that you will take our exuberance
and use it to bring light and hope
to those trapped in darkness and despair.
Use these gifts of money to empower our work
with those who have not yet seen the risen Lord
in their midst.
Use the gift of our very lives to empower our calling
to carry your Incarnate Love into the world.
We pray this with the boldness of those
who have encountered the living Christ. Amen.

SENDING FORTH

Benediction
Christ is with us in this place.
Alleluia!
Christ goes with us into the world.
Alleluia!
Go now in peace. Christ is risen!
Risen indeed! Alleluia!

CONTEMPORARY OPTIONS

Gathering Words (John 20)

Liturgist: Women, why are you weeping?
Women: **They have taken away the Lord.**
Liturgist: Men, why are you weeping?
Men: **They have taken away the Lord.**
Liturgist: Kids, why are you weeping?
Children: **They have taken away the Lord.**
Liturgist: Christ has not been taken away!
Christ is risen! Christ is alive,
here in our midst!
Everyone: **We have seen the Lord! Alleluia!**

Praise Sentences (Psalm 118)

O give thanks to the Lord, for God is good.
God's steadfast love endures forever!
There are glad songs of victory
in the tents of the righteous.
This is the Lord's doing.
It is marvelous in our eyes.
This is the day that the Lord has made.
Let us rejoice and be glad in it!

APRIL 27, 2014

Second Sunday of Easter
B. J. Beu

COLOR
White

SCRIPTURE READINGS
Acts 2:14a, 22-32; Psalm 16; 1 Peter 1:3-9; John 20:19-31

THEME IDEAS
The epistle reading promises us an imperishable inheritance through the resurrection of Jesus Christ from the dead. Each reading, in its own way, makes the bold claim: The peace of God, the divine love that is our refuge and our strength, can never be taken from us. Even when we doubt, as Thomas did, we are challenged to embrace the good news of our imperishable inheritance.

INVITATION AND GATHERING

Call to Worship (Acts 2, Psalm 16, 1 Peter 1)
Come into God's presence with joy.
**In God, we have an inheritance
that is imperishable.**
Come into God's presence with hope.
**In Christ, we have an inheritance
that cannot be defiled.**
Come into God's presence with longing.

**In the Spirit, we have an inheritance
that never fades.**
Come into God's presence with love.
**In God, we have an inheritance
that brings new life.**

Opening Prayer (Acts 2, Psalm 16, 1 Peter 1, John 20)
God of signs and wonders,
  breathe new life into us this day,
    that our spirits may awaken
      to the joy and the hope
        of our glorious inheritance
          through the living Christ.
Clear our vision, Holy One,
  that we may see the promise of Easter
    in the stirrings of this precious earth
    and in the life energy
      flowing through our bodies.
Help us find the faith to believe
  where we have not seen,
    that others may see,
      in our living and our loving,
        the glory of the risen Christ. Amen.

PROCLAMATION AND RESPONSE

Prayer of Confession (1 Peter 1, John 20)
Merciful God,
  you come offering us peace,
    but we hold onto our fears;
  you come offering us faith,
    but we cling to our doubts;
  you come offering us a future filled with promise,
    but we retreat to pleasant memories of the past.
We want to believe that you offer us an inheritance
  that is imperishable, undefiled, and unfading.
We want to see ourselves as you see us.
We want to live as you would have us live.

We want to believe that life is stronger
   than the death we see all around us.
Help our unbelief, O God,
   that we may truly know and live
      your gift of resurrection. Amen.

Words of Assurance (1 Peter 1, John 20)

The inheritance that God promises us
   is imperishable, undefiled, and unfading.
Even when we are consumed by doubt,
   God is always faithful.
Even when we lose our way,
   God is able to find us and bring us home.
Even when we are at war with ourselves,
   God is able to bring us peace.
Thanks be to God!

Passing the Peace of Christ (1 Peter 1, John 20)

When our minds churn like turbulent waters, Christ
comes to offer us peace. When our lives careen out of control like cars on a frozen highway, Christ comes to offer us
peace. Christ is here now, offering us peace. With the spirit
of Christ within us, let us turn to one another and share
signs of peace with one another.

Response to the Word (1 Peter 1, John 20)

Even though we have not seen the Lord,
we can still love him.
   Even though we cannot touch his hands,
   we can still believe.
Gathered here as the body of Christ,
and seeing Christ's love in one another,
we can say without doubt:
   We have seen the Lord!
When we witness the hands that touch us
and behold the eyes that shine Christ's love and peace,
we can proclaim with faith:
   My Lord and my God!
Do not doubt but believe.

THANKSGIVING AND COMMUNION

Invitation to the Offering (Psalm 16)

God is our chosen portion and our cup of blessing. Christ is our delight and our refuge from the storm. The Spirit has given us a goodly inheritance and blessed us with abundance. Let us share our gratitude for the grace we have received by giving freely to a world in need of Easter joy.

Offering Prayer (Psalm 16, 1 Peter 1, John 20)

O God, our refuge and our strength,
    we rejoice that you are our chosen portion,
        you are our cup that overflows to eternal life.
As we celebrate your Easter miracle
    of bringing life out of death,
        we express our gratitude and joy
            for the new life budding within us
            and all around us.
Bless the gifts we offer you this day,
    that they may bring hope and new life
        to a world that clings even now
            to the illusion of death's victory
                over the Lord of Life. Amen.

SENDING FORTH

Benediction (1 Peter 1)

Through Christ, God has given us a new birth
into a living hope.
    God has given us an inheritance
    that is imperishable, undefiled, and unfading—
    an inheritance protected by the power of God.
Rejoice, therefore, even if for a while
we suffer various trials.
    For life is stronger than death,
    love is stronger than hate,
    joy is stronger than sorrow,
    and the promises of God are sure.

CONTEMPORARY OPTIONS

Gathering Words (John 20)

Deeds of power, signs and wonders...
Christ has risen from the dead.
Blessed be the God of our Lord Jesus Christ!
Deeds of power, signs and wonders...
Christ is alive in the world!
Blessed be the God of our Lord Jesus Christ!
Deeds of power, signs and wonders...
Christ brings us peace!
Blessed be the God of our Lord Jesus Christ!

Praise Sentences (Psalm 16, 1 Peter 1)

O God, you are my chosen portion,
my cup, my bread of life.
Blessed be the God of our Lord Jesus Christ!
Blessed be the one who rose from the grave!
Blessed be the Spirit who makes us one!
O God, you are my chosen portion,
my cup, my bread of life.
Blessed be!

MAY 4, 2014

Third Sunday of Easter
Terri Stewart

COLOR

White

SCRIPTURE READINGS

Acts 2:14a, 36-41; Psalm 116:1-4, 12-19; 1 Peter 1:17-23;
Luke 24:13-35

THEME IDEAS

God's words and precepts are almost always for the community, not isolated individuals. God calls the entire community to repent, to be baptized, and to participate in God's covenant. This is especially evident in Peter's words recorded in Acts and continued in 1 Peter. We are to have love for one another through the new life born of purification and repentance. The psalmist further reminds us that calling on the name of the Lord brings salvation and new life. Then, on the road to Emmaus, two disciples reveal their hope that Jesus is the one to redeem all Israel, not them alone. They then invite Jesus into their lives because his words cause them to see things in a new way. That is the story of repentance and the cycle of salvation: an invitation for communal repentance leads to genuine love and repentance, which in turn gives us the ability to hear Jesus' invitation to new life as his words burn within our hearts.

INVITATION AND GATHERING

Call to Worship (Psalm 116)
Our God hears our prayers.
O Lord, I pray, save my life!
Our God blesses us with abundance.
O Lord, I pray, give me life!
Our God's love and covenant are steadfast and true.
O Lord, I pray, accept my sacrifice—
a sacrifice of thanksgiving, praise, and worship!

Opening Prayer (Acts 2, 1 Peter 1, Luke 24)
Fellow Traveler, you meet us as we walk the roads of life
and reveal to us mighty things.
You call us to change our lives
and to depend upon you.
You teach us the greatest, deepest mysteries,
and reveal the truth of your promised grace.
Open our ears to hear your words,
and open our hearts to burn with your truth,
that mutual love may burst forth
among all people here on earth. Amen.

PROCLAMATION AND RESPONSE

Prayer of Confession (Luke 24, Psalm 116)
Merciful God,
you walk with us,
even when we fail to see;
you call to us,
even when we fail to hear;
you listen for our petitions,
even when we fail to speak;
you whisper words of love,
even when we respond with indifference;
you call us to repentance,
even when we don't see the need.

Forgive us, Holy One.
Heal our hardness of heart,
   that we may turn to you anew.
Open our minds to your Spirit,
   that we may hear your words.
Refresh our souls,
   that we may speak of your love.
In the redeemer's name, we pray. Amen.

Words of Assurance (Acts 2, 1 Peter 1)
Our God is a redeeming God!
God's promise of redemption is for you
   and for the healing of the world,
     through the forgiveness of sins.
Rejoice and be born anew
   through the living and enduring word of God.

Passing the Peace of Christ (1 Peter 1)
With souls purified by God's redeeming love, let us offer
to one another genuine, mutual love—a love planted in
the peace of Christ, a love that fills our hearts with peace
and joy.

Response to the Word (Luke 24)
God of redeeming love,
   as we walk our own road to Emmaus:
     open the scriptures to our shut-up hearts,
     open our eyes to your vision of hope,
       that your Spirit may burn like fire
         within our souls.
Grant us the courage to respond faithfully, O God,
   that we may offer our love to one another
     and to all of your people,
       through Christ's redemptive love. Amen.

THANKSGIVING AND COMMUNION

Offering Prayer (1 Peter 1)
Gracious God,
   you have given us the gift of love:

love of you,
love of Christ,
love of one another,
love of the world.
We offer you this thanksgiving sacrifice,
that you might take it
and make this offering of love visible
for all the world to see. Amen.

Communion Liturgy (Luke 24)

Like the two disciples on the road to Emmaus,
we walk with Jesus, but do not recognize him.
Yet Jesus persists, opening our hearts to truth and love
as we share table with him.
As he gathers us close, Jesus takes the bread,
blesses it, and breaks it,
and we eat together:
you, me, and Christ at the table.
It is during the meal that we recognize Christ,
see the gift of God's love, and are transformed.
Only then can we truly say,
"The Lord has risen!"
for Christ is risen in our hearts.
Friends, loved ones, this table is prepared by Christ
for the transformation and redemption of the world.
At this table, we recognize Christ
and God's love rises in our hearts.
Come, let us break bread with the One
who is present now.

SENDING FORTH

Benediction (Luke 24, 1 Peter 1)

May Christ's love fill you this day
with the living and enduring word of God.
May Christ's love lift you up and guide you,
that you may go forth to transform the world.
Shalom and amen.

CONTEMPORARY OPTIONS

Gathering Words (Psalm 116, Acts 2, 1 Peter 1)

God listens.
> **Call on God!**

God saves.
> **Call on God!**

God redeems.
> **Call on God!**

God loves.
> **Call on God!**

Praise Sentences (Luke 24)

Jesus walks with us, even when we don't know it.
Jesus talks with us, even when we can't understand.
Jesus eats with us and offers life to us.
Jesus opens our eyes and our hearts to the glory of God.
Praise to Christ, who is with us!

MAY 11, 2014

Fourth Sunday of Easter, Festival of the Christian Home/Mother's Day

Mary J. Scifres

COLOR

White

SCRIPTURE READINGS

Acts 2:42-47; Psalm 23; 1 Peter 2:19-25; John 10:1-10

THEME IDEAS

The shepherd who gives us life, who restores our lives, who saves our lives, is also the shepherd who guides us, redirects us when we go astray, and calls us to fullness of life. So often, shepherding images for Christ are gentle and sweet, but these scriptures remind us that shepherding God's followers is a challenging task...and living as the sheep of Christ's fold is not an easy journey of discipleship. But when we devote ourselves to the teachings of our faith, to the fellowship of our faith communities, and to the mutual support of our communities through prayer, sharing, and giving, we find that indeed, we "shall not want." We have everything we need as we live in this fold, travel on this journey, and live into the fullness of life offered by Christ.

INVITATION AND GATHERING

Call to Worship (Acts 2, John 10, Mother's Day)

Christ, our shepherd, calls us here.
God's gate of love has swung wide!
Jesus, our brother, welcomes us home.
The family of God embraces us all.
Our mothering God invites us with love.
For we are all precious sheep in God's pasture.

Opening Prayer (Acts 2, Psalm 23, John 10)

God of love and grace,
 as you swing wide the gate of welcome this day,
  strengthen us to walk through the gate
   of your love and mercy.
Protect us from harm
 as we lie down in the fields of your mercy
  and rise again to travel this journey of faith.
Speak to us through your teachings this day,
 that we may devote ourselves to your guidance
  and feed on your life-giving word.
In the beloved name of Jesus, our shepherd,
 we pray. Amen.

PROCLAMATION AND RESPONSE

Prayer of Confession (Acts 2, Psalm 23, 1 Peter 2)

Even as the wounds of Jesus
 remind us of the healing and the hope
  Christ offers us this Easter season,
   we face our own wounds
    and fall into doubt and despair.
Help us face the realities
 that separate us from you
  and from one another, O God.
Guide our feet onto paths of health and wholeness,
 that we may walk closely with you
  and with those who love and care for us.

Words of Assurance (1 Peter 2, John 10)

Even those who have gone astray like lost sheep
    are welcomed back into the loving arms
    of Christ our shepherd, the guardian of our souls.
Rejoice! For all are welcome into God's grace
    through the gate of the shepherd's love.

Passing the Peace of Christ (Acts 2, John 10)

Rejoice! You who have walked through the gate of God's love are gifts of love to others. Let us share our gift of love as we greet our neighbors with signs of peace and compassion.

Response to the Word (Psalm 23)

The Lord is my shepherd.
    I shall not want.
Christ walks with me on quiet days of peace.
    The shepherd abides with me
    on difficult journeys of sorrow.
But the Lord is also our shepherd.
    We shall not want.
Our lives overflow with God's love.
    Thanks be to God!

Litany of Love: A Prayer of Thanksgiving (Mother's Day)

For shepherds and mentors, mothers and guides,
    we give thanks and praise this day.
For friends who care, for families who nurture,
    we give thanks and praise this day.
For this family of faith, for spiritual teachers,
    we give thanks and praise this day.
For the gift of love, both given and received,
    we give thanks and praise this day.

THANKSGIVING AND COMMUNION

Invitation to the Offering (Acts 2, Psalm 23)

All that we have, and all that we need, is God's—

gifts to be shared with one another,
as we live in the abundance of God's love.
As the family of God, as the sheep of Christ's pasture,
we offer God's gifts for all.

Offering Prayer (Acts 2, 1 Peter 2)
As we offer these gifts to you, Shepherd of our souls,
we thank you for the love
flowing through our lives
and through these gifts.
May they be filled with your awesome power,
that through these gifts,
many signs and wonders will be done.
May no one be in need,
and may your community of love
be established upon this earth.
In your holy name, we pray. Amen.

SENDING FORTH

Benediction (Psalm 23)
The Lord is our shepherd and goes with us now.
With souls restored and lives renewed,
our cups overflow!
Surely goodness and mercy shall follow us home.
We go forth with God's love for all!

CONTEMPORARY OPTIONS

Gathering Words (Acts 2, Psalm 23)
Whether shepherd, coach, teacher, parent...
Christ walks with us all the way.
In lovely fields and in caves of despair,
Christ walks with us all the way.
With guiding hands and teaching words,
Christ walks with us all the way.
In the community of faith and on lonely roads,
Christ walks with us all the way.

Come, my friends, to worship and praise!
Christ walks with us all the way.

Praise Sentences (Psalm 23, John 10)
God our shepherd is always there.
God is with us now!
Christ our guide is always there.
God is with us now!

MAY 18, 2014

Fifth Sunday of Easter
Deborah Sokolove

COLOR
White

SCRIPTURE READINGS
Acts 7:55-60; Psalm 31:1-5, 15-16; 1 Peter 2:2-10;
John 14:1-14

THEME IDEAS
Jesus shows us what God is really like, inviting us to follow him into fullness of life. In this new life, we become
living stones, built into a spiritual house that no one can
destroy; we become a holy priesthood, proclaiming the
truth of Christ; we are transformed into God's own people, that we might extend the loving-kindness of God to
the world.

INVITATION AND GATHERING

Call to Worship (1 Peter 2, John 14)
Jesus calls us to follow him.
   We come wondering where he will take us.
Jesus shows us the way to God.
   He is the way, the truth, and the life.
Jesus prepares a place for us in the house of God.
   We come like living stones,

ready to be built into a spiritual house,
a welcoming home for all who seek the Holy One.

Opening Prayer (Acts 7, Psalm 31, John 14)
Holy, merciful, builder of eternity,
    you have filled us with the desire to know you,
        and to live in the refuge of your embrace.
You have shown us your face
    in the face of Jesus, your holy Child,
        the one who has promised
            to do whatever we ask in his name.
Fill us with your Holy Spirit,
    that we may stand like your servant, Stephen,
        as witnesses to your love. Amen.

PROCLAMATION AND RESPONSE

Prayer of Confession (Acts 7, Psalm 31, 1 Peter 2)
Holy redeemer of all who are in trouble,
    we cower in fear, unwilling to place our trust
        in your promised deliverance.
    Trusting our own strength,
        we are unwilling to seek refuge in you.
We hide our eyes,
    unwilling to see your face shining upon us
        in the faces of our neighbors.
    We cover our ears,
        unwilling to hear your good news
            in stories told by others.
We want to throw stones at those who challenge us
    to learn something new.
    Forgive our weakness, Holy One,
        for refusing to do your will.

Words of Assurance (Psalm 31)
The Holy One is a rock of refuge,
    a strong fortress in times of trial.
God does not hold our weakness against us,
    but fills us with the Holy Spirit to be our strength.

In the name of Christ, you are forgiven.
In the name of Christ, you are forgiven.
Glory to God. Amen.

Passing the Peace of Christ (John 14)
Jesus assures us that as he is in God, so we are in Christ.
The peace of Christ be in you and with you.
The peace of Christ be in you and with you.

Prayer of Preparation (1 Peter 2)
Holy One, you invite us to taste your goodness,
    and to come before you like newborn infants
        who are hungry for your word.
Open our ears and our hearts,
    that we might be nourished
        with the knowledge
            that we are your people,
            and you are our God.

Response to the Word (1 Peter 2)
In Christ, we become a royal priesthood,
    a holy nation, God's own people,
    proclaiming the good news
    of God's loving-kindness and grace.

THANKSGIVING AND COMMUNION

Invitation to the Offering (John 14)
Let us bring our gifts and offerings for the many dwelling
places of the Holy One.

Offering Prayer (1 Peter 2)
Holy Giver of all that is good,
    receive these offerings from our hands.
Use us as living stones,
    building your house
        in the hearts of your people.

—OR—

Offering Prayer (Psalm 31, 1 Peter 2)
God of overflowing abundance,

you have fed us on your spiritual milk
   and nourished us on your heavenly food.
When the snares of this world
   threatened to overwhelm us,
      you have been our fortress and our rock,
         saving us from the net that is hidden from us.
Thankful for the mercy we have received,
   we entrust our lives and our spirits into your care,
      offering you our gifts,
         in the hope that they may reflect your light
            for all to see. Amen.

(B. J. Beu)

Great Thanksgiving
Christ be with you.
   And also with you.
Lift up your hearts.
   We lift them up to God.
Let us give our thanks to the Holy One.
   It is right to give our thanks and praise.

It is a right, good, and joyful thing,
   always and everywhere to give our thanks to you—
   you who have called us to be your people,
   and have invited us to live in your eternal presence.
We give you thanks for your holy witness, Stephen,
   who trusted in your loving-kindness,
   and asked you to forgive his enemies,
   following the example of Jesus,
   in whose face we see your face.
And so, with your creatures on earth,
   and all the heavenly chorus,
   we praise your name and join their unending hymn:
   Holy, holy, holy Lord, God of power and might,
      heaven and earth are full of your glory.
   Hosanna in the highest. Blessed is the one
      who comes in the name of the Lord.
   Hosanna in the highest.

Holy are you, and holy is your child, Jesus Christ,
   who is the way, the truth, and the life,
   the one who shows us fullness of life in your Spirit.

On the night in which he gave himself up,
   Jesus took bread, gave thanks to you,
   broke the bread, and gave it to the disciples, saying:
   "Take, eat; this is my body which is given for you.
   Do this in remembrance of me."
When the supper was over, Jesus took the cup,
   offered thanks, and gave it to the disciples, saying:
   "Drink from this, all of you;
   this is my life in the new covenant,
   poured out for you and for many,
   for the forgiveness of sins.
   Do this, as often as you drink it,
   in remembrance of me."
And so, in remembrance of your mighty acts
   in Jesus Christ . . . we proclaim the mystery of faith.
   Christ has died.
   Christ is risen.
   Christ will come again.

Pour out your Holy Spirit on us gathered here,
   and on these gifts of bread and wine.
Make them be for us the body and blood of Christ,
   that we may be the body of Christ
   to a broken, hurting world.
Rock of Refuge, Redeemer of the broken, Spirit of Life,
   we praise your holy, eternal name. **Amen.**

SENDING FORTH

Benediction (Acts 7, Psalm 31, 1 Peter 2)
   Go into the world as the people of God,
      sharing the loving-kindness
      that you have received from God
      and the abundant grace of the Holy Spirit

through Jesus, who is the Christ.
Amen.

CONTEMPORARY OPTIONS

Gathering Words (1 Peter 2, John 14)
Do not let your hearts be troubled.
Believe in God, believe also in me.
We come like living stones,
ready to be built into a spiritual house—
a welcoming home for all who seek the Holy One.

Praise Sentences
Rock of Refuge, Redeemer of the broken, Spirit of Life,
we praise your holy, eternal name.

—OR—

Praise Sentences (1 Peter 2)
Christ is our living rock!
Worship the cornerstone of our faith.
Christ is our rock!
Christ is our rock!
Christ is our rock!

(B. J. Beu)

MAY 25, 2014

Sixth Sunday of Easter

B. J. Beu

COLOR
White

SCRIPTURE READINGS
Acts 17:22-31; Psalm 66:8-20; 1 Peter 3:13-22;
John 14:15-21

THEME IDEAS
Love and suffering seem to be the two great paths to God.
Suffering gets our attention, and love shows us the nature
of God. The psalmist speaks of being tested and tried as
silver is tried—God put other nations over Israel to lead
them through fire and water into a spacious place of blessing. The epistle speaks of the suffering that will come from
following Christ and urges the people to do good works
anyway—for it is better to suffer for doing good than for
doing evil. In the Gospel reading, Jesus promises the disciples that he will not leave them comfortless, but will
send them the Advocate, the Holy Spirit, to teach them
the truth about God and holy love. The reading from Acts
does not fit this theme, but recounts the story of Paul in
the Areopagus, proclaiming the God of Jesus Christ as the
one the Athenians worshiped as an unknown god. Acts
and the epistle also share the theme of searching and
groping for God and ultimate truth.

INVITATION AND GATHERING

Call to Worship (Acts 17, Psalm 66, John 14)

Search for God, you seekers of the way.
Grope for truth, you disciples of wisdom.
Where shall we go to find what we seek?
And where shall we look for answers?
Come to the fountain of grace
and find what you are looking for.
Look inside, for in God we live and move
and have our being.
Our poets and artists proclaim boldly
that we are children of God. Can it be?
We are God's offspring, God's beloved.
God is in us and we are in God.
How can this be?
This is a hard truth to believe.
Wait patiently for the Advocate, the Spirit of truth,
who will reveal these mysteries and the love of God.
We will wait in hope and love.

Opening Prayer (Psalm 66, 1 Peter 3, John 14)

Refiner's Fire,
purify our lives
like precious silver,
that our hearts may be made ready
to receive all the love you offer.
Burn away our fears
and our instincts for revenge,
that we may go through fire
and the water of our baptism
and come out the other side
abiding in your truth.
In times of suffering
return us to thoughts of you
and your commandment to love one another,
that everything we do
may be honorable and just.
In your Holy name, we pray. Amen.

PROCLAMATION AND RESPONSE

Prayer of Confession (Acts 17, 1 Peter 3, John 14)
Eternal God, in our searching and groping to find you,
  we have settled for idols
    made of gold, silver, and stone.
We have put our faith in our money,
  placed our hope in institutions of brick and mortar,
    and trusted our weapons of war to keep us safe.
We have sought after our own comfort and ease,
  rejected calls for personal and national sacrifice,
    and belittled calls challenging us to aim higher.
Forgive us.
Help us give an accounting
  of the hope that is in us—
    the hope nurtured by our life in Christ,
    the hope found in your commandment of love,
    the hope that comes from being your offspring
      and abiding in your Spirit. Amen.

Assurance of Pardon (Psalm 66)
Even when our world falls apart and we find ourselves
  journeying through fire and water,
    God leads us back and brings us to a spacious place
    of laughter and light.
The One who is faithful, the One who abides in us,
  forgives our missteps and leads us home.
  Thanks be to God!

Invitation to the Word (Acts 17, John 14)
Spirit of truth, as we grope for you in the dark,
  come to us and illumine our path.
Surround us with your love,
  and strengthen us with your grace,
    that our hearts and minds
      may be open to listen for your word
      and to live your love.

Response to the Word (John 14:21)

Take heart in the words of Christ:

"Whoever has my commandments and keeps them loves me. Whoever loves me will be loved by my [Mother and] Father, and I will love them and reveal myself to them."

This is the word of God for the people of God.

Thanks be to God.

THANKSGIVING AND COMMUNION

Invitation to the Offering

As lovers of God, let us be more than hearers of the word, let us be doers of the word also. Through our love for others, we keep God's commandments and abide in the living God. Let us open ourselves now to the joy of sharing in the love of God as we express our love and concern for God's world.

Offering Prayer (Psalm 66, 1 Peter 3)

Healing God,
when we went astray,
you purified us with fire
and washed us clean
in the waters of our baptism.
In gratitude and thanks,
for your constant care and your many blessings,
we return these gifts to you,
that they may be used
to bring hope and light
to a world in need. Amen.

SENDING FORTH

Benediction (Acts 17, John 14)

Once we searched and groped for God in the darkness.
**Now we reside in glorious light,
knowing that God goes with us.**
Once we wandered with the delusion

that God was far from us.
Now we abide in the truth:
In God we live and move and have our being.
Once, we felt isolated and alone.
Now we know that the Advocate,
the Spirit of truth, guides our hearts and minds,
dwelling within us, in communion with God
and with one another.

CONTEMPORARY OPTIONS

Gathering Words (Acts 17, John 14)
Gather us in, God of love.
Blessed be God,
who calls us to love.
Gather us in, God of love.
Blessed be Christ,
who shows us the way.
Gather us in, God of love.
Blessed be the Spirit of truth,
who reveals fullness of life.
Gather us in, God of love,
and be with us as we worship.

Praise Sentences (Psalm 66, John 14)
Bless our God, sisters and brothers in Christ.
Sound God's praise.
Bless our God, all who search for truth.
Sanctify Christ as Lord.
Bless our God, pilgrims of the way.
Shout God's holy name.

MAY 29, 2014

Ascension Day
B. J. Beu

COLOR
White

SCRIPTURE READINGS
Acts 1:1-11; Psalm 47; Ephesians 1:15-23; Luke 24:44-53

THEME IDEAS
Ascension Day is about a power that lies beyond our ordinary existence. Through the same power that raised Jesus from the dead and heals our bodies and our souls, we receive the gifts of the Holy Spirit. As Jesus is lifted up to the heavens, we are reminded to look beyond earthly power to the power of the Most High God.

INVITATION AND GATHERING

Call to Worship (Psalm 47)
Clap your hands, people of God.
    Shout to God with cries of joy.
Sing your praises, people of God.
    Sing praises to our king, sing praises.
Look to the heavens, people of God.
    See the power of the Most High God.
Clap your hands, people of God.
    Shout to God with cries of joy.

Opening Prayer (Acts 1, Luke 24)
Most High God,
    as Christ ascended into the heavens,
        may our hearts ascend to you.
Open our eyes to the power of your Spirit,
    that we may strive for more
        than the pedestrian ways of this world.
Open our lives to the fullness of your power,
    that we may be clothed with power from on high.
Help us wait patiently for the baptism of your Spirit,
    that we may be found worthy of your great gifts. Amen.

PROCLAMATION AND RESPONSE

Prayer of Confession (Acts 1, Ephesians 1, Luke 24)
Merciful God, when offered the promise
    of your glorious inheritance,
        we settle for so much less.
Rather than lifting our gaze to see and live
    with the eyes of our hearts enlightened,
        our eyes are fixed on the ground;
        our hearts are set on earthly power;
        our aspirations are limited to getting ahead.
Forgive us.
Teach us anew to wait for your Holy Spirit,
    that we may be clothed with power from on high,
        in the name of the one who ascended to heaven
            to show us the way to live here on earth.

Assurance of Pardon (Acts 1, Ephesians 1, Luke 24)
When we have the courage to wait,
    in patient emptiness, for your Spirit, O God,
    you justify the hope to which we have been called,
    you fill us with your Spirit,
    you forgive our transgressions,
        and you clothe us with power from on high.

Response to the Word (Ephesians 1:17-19)

Hear anew these words of Paul: "I pray that the God of our Lord Jesus Christ, the [God] of glory, will give you a spirit of wisdom and revelation that makes God known to you. I pray that the eyes of your heart will have enough light to see what is the hope of God's call, what is the richness of God's glorious inheritance among believers, and what is the overwhelming greatness of God's power that is working among us believers. This power is conferred by the energy of God's powerful strength."

THANKSGIVING AND COMMUNION

Offering Prayer (Psalm 47)

O God, we praise you for your power and might;
we praise you for your love and mercy;
we praise you for giving us your Spirit;
we praise you for your every blessing.
In gratitude and thanksgiving
for all we have received from your hand,
we return to you the fruit of our industry.
This we pray,
in the name of the one who ascended to heaven,
that we might have fullness of life
here on earth. Amen.

SENDING FORTH

Benediction (Luke 24)

Lift up your eyes to the heavens.
Christ ascended to show us the way.
Trust in the power of the Spirit.
Christ ascended to clothe us with power.
Go as witnesses of the risen Lord.
Christ ascended to bring us eternal life.

CONTEMPORARY OPTIONS

Gathering Words (Acts 1, Luke 24)

Are you ready to receive the Spirit?
When will it come?
God alone appoints the time.
We are ready.
Are you ready to be clothed with power from on high?
We are ready.
Look to Christ, who calls us to wait and be ready.
We are ready.

Praise Sentences (Psalm 47)

Sing praises to God, sing praises.
Sing praises to our king, sing praises.
Our God is king over all the earth.
Sing praises with shouts of joy, sing praises.
Sing praises to God, sing praises.
Sing praises to our king, sing praises.

JUNE 1, 2014

Seventh Sunday of Easter, Proper 4

B. J. Beu

COLOR
White

SCRIPTURE READINGS
Acts 1:6-14; Psalm 68:1-10, 32-35; 1 Peter 4:12-14; 5:6-11; John 17:1-11

THEME IDEAS
The theme of restoration unifies these readings. In Acts, the disciples ask Jesus if it is the time when he will restore the kingdom to Israel. The psalmist extols God as the Father of orphans and the protector of widows—the One who restores the fortunes of the weak, the One who provides for the needy. The epistle exhorts the faithful to bear their suffering a while longer, for God will "restore, support, strengthen, and establish" them in due course (5:10 NRSV). In the Gospel, Jesus assures the faithful that they no longer need restoration, for he will glorify them as God has glorified him. Indeed, the point of restoration is summed up in Jesus' hope that we may all be one, as he and God, his Mother and Father, are one.

INVITATION AND GATHERING

Call to Worship (Psalm 68)
Let the earth quake.
Let the heavens pour down rain

in the presence of our mighty God.
Let the wicked flee
like smoke in a mighty wind.
Let the unrighteous tremble and shake
like thunder in the mountains.
For God, the Father of orphans,
the Mother and protector of widows,
rescues the perishing,
but sends the rebellious to a parched land.
Sing to God, O kingdoms of the earth.
Sing praises to our God.
Awesome is our God in the sanctuary of heaven.
Awesome is the One who gives power to the people.
Blessed be the Lord, the God of Israel.
God is greatly to be praised.

Opening Prayer (Psalm 68, 1 Peter 4)
O rider in the heavens,
bear us on the winds of your mercy
as we are cast about by the storms of life.
Grant us the strength to persevere in times of trial,
that we may be glad and shout for joy
when Christ's glory is revealed.
Keep us safe from our adversaries,
who are like roaring lions
seeking someone to devour
in their love of carnage.
Restore us, support us, strengthen us,
and establish us as your people, Holy One,
that we may bear witness
to your glorious power,
through Jesus Christ, our Lord.

PROCLAMATION AND RESPONSE

Prayer of Confession (Acts 1, John 17)
Bringer of glory, author of everlasting life,
when Jesus' disciples watched
as their friend and teacher

was carried away to heaven,
 they felt bereft and alone.
In your mercy, you sent angels to comfort them.
We too need your winged messengers of hope, O God,
 for we also feel bereft and alone.
We long to be like Peter, James and John,
 and Mary the mother of Jesus,
 who devoted themselves to prayer.
But in our isolation,
 we forsake community,
 and resign ourselves to loneliness and loss.
Teach us once more that we are yours
 and that you are ours.
Remind us again
 that eternal life comes
 from knowing you
 and being known by you.
Open us to prayer.
Open us to hope.
Open us to life in your holy name. Amen.

Words of Assurance (Acts 1, Psalm 68)

The Father of orphans, the Mother and protector
 of widows, provides a home for the desolate.
How much more have we received in Christ,
 we who have been blessed with the Holy Spirit?
Rejoice, sisters and brothers in Christ!
It is God's good pleasure to give us the kingdom.

Response to the Word (Acts 1, John 17)

Do not look up wondering where Christ has gone.
Christ is all around you:
 in the carefree laughter of our children;
 in the forgiving smiles of our elders;
 in the heart that gives and receives love.
We all belong to God,
 because we belong to Christ
 and Christ belongs to God.

Live into this good news,
    and you will taste eternal life,
        each and every day.

THANKSGIVING AND COMMUNION

Offering Prayer (Psalm 68)
    God of overflowing abundance,
        in times of drought,
            you kiss the earth with rain,
                renewing the life of every living thing;
        in times of hardship and want,
            you restore the fortunes of your people,
                giving them a goodly heritage.
    In tribute and thanks for your many blessings,
        we bring you gifts of our time, talents, and treasures,
            that the world might be touched by your love. Amen.

SENDING FORTH

Benediction (1 Peter 4:13-14; 5:6)
    Rejoice when you share in Christ's suffering,
        for you will be glad and shout for joy
        when Christ's glory is revealed.
    Take heart when you are reviled for doing good works
        in Christ's name, because the Spirit of God,
        the spirit of glory, is resting upon you.
    Humble yourself under the mighty hand of God,
        that the Lord may lift you up in due time.

CONTEMPORARY OPTIONS

Gathering Words (Psalm 68)
    Let the righteous be joyful.
    Let the faithful sing and shout for joy.
        Sing to the Lord all the earth.
        Let everything that draws breath
        sing to the Lord.

Let the righteous be joyful.
Let the faithful sing and shout for joy.
**Let all people draw near
and worship the Lord!**

Praise Sentences (Psalm 68, 1 Peter 4)
Mighty is our God and greatly to be praised.
**To God be the power and the glory
forever and ever.**
Blessed be our God.
Blessed be our God.
Blessed be our God.

JUNE 8, 2014

Pentecost Sunday, Proper 5

J. Wayne Pratt

COLOR

Red

SCRIPTURE READINGS

Acts 2:1-21; Psalm 104:24-34, 35b; 1 Corinthians 12:3b-13; John 7:37-39

THEME IDEAS

Wind and fire, discordant voices and languages, vivid dreams and visions, and an outpouring of the Holy Spirit establish the inauguration of an entirely new era. With the ushering in of the Holy Spirit, the disciples are empowered to proclaim the gospel of the risen Christ. The Apostle Peter captures the moment and preaches to the crowd, witnessing to the death and resurrection of Jesus Christ and to the forgiveness of sins. Through word and sacrament, the Holy Spirit enables us to believe in and proclaim Christ as our savior. Pentecost, and its celebratory nature, calls us to move from our safe, convenient "upper rooms" into the world around us—a world that thirsts for a redeeming word and a loving gesture. Through the gift of the Holy Spirit, the church is invited to celebrate this day with great joy and thanksgiving.

INVITATION AND GATHERING

Call to Worship (John 7, Acts 2)

A new era has dawned:
an era ushered in by God's Holy Spirit,
an era heralded by rushing wind and flames of fire.
Unfamiliar voices startle our expectations.
God has sent the Holy Spirit to lead us onward.
The Spirit comes and we are transformed.
A new age has begun.
Praise God for new life!
Praise God for the birth of the church,
born of the power of the Holy Spirit!

Opening Prayer (Acts 2, 1 Corinthians 12)

O Lord, our God,
pour out your Holy Spirit once again,
that the world may know
the gifts and blessing of your power.
Take away our confusion
and grant us clarity of vision.
Open our senses
to the mystery and wonder of faith.
Open our minds
to the signs of hope you seek to share with us.
We are indeed your church,
called together in one place
for praise and thanksgiving.
Let your Holy Spirit fill this sanctuary
and sanctify our lives. Amen.

PROCLAMATION AND RESPONSE

Prayer of Confession (Acts 2, Psalm 104)

Gracious and Almighty God,
we have often failed to be receptive
to the power of your Holy Spirit.

149

Fearful of true unity,
    our words have often confused rather than clarified,
        hurt rather than healed,
            and divided rather than united your people.
In your never failing grace,
    bestow the wondrous gift of your Spirit among us.
Forgive us when we turn away
    from oneness and wholeness,
        and save us from the terrible toll
            of apathy and neglect.
May we constantly sing your praises,
    honoring Father, Son, and Holy Spirit,
        one God, Mother and Father of us all. Amen.

Assurance of Pardon

There is no fear, confusion, hurt, or division
    that cannot be bridged by God's Holy Spirit
    or that cannot be transformed
    in the name of Jesus Christ.
The generous outpouring of the Spirit
    moves through the people of God
    like an everflowing river,
    washing away sin, and bringing forth unity.
Thanks be to God.

Response to the Word

With hope and joy,
    we have heard your word, O God.
As people of Pentecost,
    may we each be filled with wonder and delight,
    may we each claim our heritage
        as people of wind and fire.
Filled with the Spirit,
    may our hearts and minds be transformed
        to dream dreams and see visions,
            that we might sing your praises
                and do your will. Amen.

THANKSGIVING AND COMMUNION

Offering Prayer (Acts 2)

O God of all creation,
 we gather on this Pentecost Sunday
  to celebrate the outpouring of your love
   and the grace-filled gift of your Holy Spirit.
As your Spirit moves among us and through us,
 encourage our generosity and thankfulness
  in the sharing of our tithes and offerings.
We ask this in the name of Christ Jesus,
 whose promise of the Spirit fulfills our lives. Amen.

Communion Prayer (John 7, Acts 2, Psalm 104)

Come, Holy Spirit, come!
Come now and be among us,
 filling this bread and this cup with your presence,
  that we might more fully know you
   as we share in this meal.
As we break bread together,
 and as we lift the cup of blessing,
  may the winds and flames
   of renewal and transformation
    move our hearts to receive your joy.
Make us like cleansing rivers of living water
 as we encounter people of every nation
  in Christ's name. Amen.

SENDING FORTH

Benediction (Acts 2, 1 Corinthians 12)

Go now as children of God.
Go into the world as those who are set free
 by the rushing winds and blazing fires of the Spirit.
Go now in the name of God who creates us;
 in the name of Christ Jesus who redeems us;
 and in the name of the Holy Spirit
  who counsels and guides us.

Go and share the gifts of the Holy Spirit.
Go now to peace. Amen.

CONTEMPORARY OPTIONS

Gathering Words

Do you hear the wind rushing among us?
**It sounds like discordant voices
shouting to be heard.**
Do you see the flames licking at your feet?
They dance about as if inciting us to move.
Rejoice in the signs of God's Spirit.
Sing praises to the Almighty One.

Praise Sentences (1 Corinthians 12, Acts 2)

Although many and diverse,
we gather as one body in Christ.
**Together in unity, we praise God
for the gift of the Holy Spirit.**
By God's gracious love, we are one in the Spirit.
**We are all baptized into one body,
and made to drink of one Spirit.**
Everyone who calls on the name of the Lord
shall be saved.
Everyone?
Yes, everyone!

JUNE 15, 2014

Trinity Sunday, Father's Day
Bill Hoppe

COLOR
White

SCRIPTURE READINGS
Genesis 1:1–2:4a; Psalm 8; 2 Corinthians 13:11-13; Matthew 28:16-20

THEME IDEAS
From the beginning to the ending of existence, God's unselfish bounty and purposes are shown in each of today's scriptures. The Trinity is present in each moment of creation, making humankind in God's image and likeness. In pondering the infinite wonders of the universe, the psalmist is overwhelmed by God's majesty and by God's care for each one of us. We are empowered with all authority in heaven and on earth by the Creator, Christ, and Holy Spirit to bring God's peace and love to all: in discipleship, baptism, and teaching. Grace, love, and communion abound in God's presence.

INVITATION AND GATHERING

Call to Worship (Genesis 1–2, Psalm 8)
In the beginning, on the first day,
before anything existed, God spoke:

"Let there be light!" And there was light.
And God saw that it was good.
On the second day, before the cosmos existed,
God spoke, calling the sky into being.
And it was so. And God saw that it was good.
On the third day, before the waters were gathered
into the seas, God spoke, calling forth the dry land:
"Let the Earth produce growth, and fruit trees
of every kind!" And God saw that it was good.
On the fourth day, before night was separate from day,
God spoke, calling forth the sun, moon, and stars:
"Let there be lights in the heavens!"
And God saw that it was good.
On the fifth day, before life burst forth from the seas
and from the skies, God spoke:
"Let there be fish that swim and birds that fly!"
And God saw that it was good.
On the sixth day, before animals walked abroad,
God spoke, calling forth animals and humans:
"Let there be creatures of every kind!
Let humankind appear in our image!"
On the seventh day, God rested.
God saw all that was made and called it very good!
O Lord our God, how glorious is your name!
How majestic are your works!

Opening Prayer (Matthew 28)
Holy One,
    you have called us to become vessels of your love—
        living examples of your peace
            in this harsh and fearful world.
We hear your call to share the good news
    of Christ's love:
        in deed and in truth,
        in acts of justice and righteousness,
        in words of mercy and compassion.
For this we were created.
For this we are called to serve.

May our lives shine the light of love—
    the light of that first moment of creation,
    the light of servant love.
Go with us; live through us; and stay with us,
    now and forevermore. Amen.

PROCLAMATION AND RESPONSE

Prayer of Confession (Genesis 1–2, Psalm 8)
Creator God,
    what are we that you should take notice of us;
    who are we that you should love us so completely?
You have created us from the stuff of stars,
    from the building blocks of the universe.
You have given us a world in which to live,
    a home in which to breathe and grow.
How carelessly and callously
    have we treated your creation and one another.
In our arrogance, we have lost sight of the goodness
    you infused into this amazing existence.
Help us hear your voice anew:
    in the simplicity of a child's laughter,
    in the sound of the wind moving through the trees.
As we gaze at the majesty of the moon and the stars
    and the wonders of the heavens,
        may we see your purpose in our lives. Amen.

Words of Assurance (Genesis 1–2, Psalm 8)
From the dust of the earth, we were formed.
With the breath that God breathed into us,
    we live and know the power of love.
All that God has created, the Lord has called good.
How majestic is the name of the Lord in all the earth!

Passing the Peace of Christ (2 Corinthians 13)
Love one another, live together in peace, and the God of
love and peace will be with you and dwell within your
hearts. God's people wait to greet you in grace and fellowship, that all may share in the deep peace of the Spirit.
Share the peace of Christ with one another.

Response to the Word (Matthew 28)

By your power and authority, Lord,
　　may your servant love become our way of life,
　　may your grace and forgiveness inspire us
　　　　to teach this desperate world hope for the future.
May we become the living embodiment
　　of your good news,
　　　　in all that we say and do.
In the midst of our fears and doubts,
　　help us to take heart—
　　　　for nothing in heaven or on earth
　　　　　　can stand against your love.
Surrounding us with your constant presence,
　　you are with us always, as you promised,
　　　　from the beginning to the end,
　　　　　　to life's close and completion.

THANKSGIVING AND COMMUNION

Offering Prayer (Genesis 1–2, Psalm 8)

Everywhere we look, and everywhere we turn,
　　all that you have set before us,
　　all that you surround us with
　　　　is good, sustaining, sufficient, and complete.
What indescribable joy and delight
　　is evident in the works of your hands!
We rejoice with you and celebrate your creation,
　　as we freely return to you
　　　　what you have so selflessly given to us.
We worship you and we praise you, O God. Amen!

SENDING FORTH

Benediction (2 Corinthians 13, Matthew 28)

May the grace of Christ keep you in harmony
　　with one another.
May the love of God keep you in peace.

May the presence of the Lord surround you
   with the communion of the Holy Spirit.
From before the beginning of all things,
   to the farthest reaches beyond the end of time
   the Lord is with you always. Amen!

CONTEMPORARY OPTIONS

Gathering Words (Genesis 1–2)
   Earth and moon, sun and stars:
   All is good!
   Day and night, light and dark:
   All is good!
   Plants and trees, fish and birds:
   All is good!
   Animals and humans, life everywhere:
   All is good! All is good!

Praise Sentences (Genesis 1–2, Psalm 8, Matthew 28)
   We are made in God's image.
   We are made in God's likeness!
   All of creation, all that is known and unknown...
   God has shared with us!
   God's love sustains us.
   God's presence surrounds us!
   We are baptized in God's name.
   We are immersed in God's love!

JUNE 22, 2014

Second Sunday after Pentecost, Proper 7

Mary J. Scifres

COLOR

Green

SCRIPTURE READINGS

Genesis 21:8-21; Psalm 86:1-10, 16-17; Romans 6:1b-11; Matthew 10:24-39

THEME IDEAS

As we leave the Easter-Pentecost cycle behind, we turn to the Ordinary Season of lections that are chosen chronologically, rather than thematically. Each week, the Psalm will relate to the lesson from the Hebrew Scriptures. The Epistle readings will take us through Paul's letter to the church in Rome, and the Gospel lessons will take us chronologically through Matthew's account of Jesus' life and ministry. Today's readings, disparate though they may be, all hold a sense of irony as fortunes are reversed, opposites are lifted up, and harsh realities are held in tension with the hope and trust we strive to proclaim as people of faith. Our yearning to be heard by God amidst deep anguish is reflected in Hagar's story.

INVITATION AND GATHERING

Call to Worship (Psalm 86)
Lift up your voice.
God hears the cry of the faithful.
Sing praise to Christ.
Christ's name is worthy of praise.
Turn now to God.
God awaits us here.

Opening Prayer (Genesis 21, Psalm 86)
Holy One,
come to us now.
Be present in our worship
and in our lives.
Hear our cries,
and speak to our souls.
Give us your strength,
that we may live all the days of our lives
in steadfast faith and hope.

PROCLAMATION AND RESPONSE

Prayer of Confession (Genesis 21, Psalm 86)
O God, hearken to our need.
So often when we cry to you,
we do not hear your voice.
Too often when we look for you,
we fail to see you in our lives.
We know the depths of despair
and the anguish of loneliness.
Teach us the joy of hope fulfilled,
the comfort of companionship offered.
Pour over us with your steadfast love,
and shower us with your constant presence.
Be present in our lives and in our world,
that we may truly know that we are not alone,
that you are fully in our midst,
and that we need not be afraid. Amen.

Words of Assurance (Genesis 21, Psalm 86)

Do not be afraid: God has heard your cries,
  knows your voice, and calls your name.
Do not be afraid: God is with us—
  loving us and holding us close,
  all the days of our lives.

Passing the Peace of Christ

Hold one another close, that in this fellowship, we may know the presence of God. Share signs of God's love as you pass the peace of Christ this day.

Introduction to the Word (Genesis 21, Psalm 86)

Even as we seek to be heard, God yearns to speak to us. Incline your ear. Listen for the word of God.

Response to the Word (Genesis 21, Psalm 86)

Like Hagar before us, we have known times of despair.
  Crying out to God, we yearn to be heard,
  we ache to be helped.
Lift your voice to the Lord, and trust that God will hear and respond to your pleas.
(A time of reflection may follow. Invite people to reflect on times of despair in a way appropriate to your congregation. In pairs, people may share a struggle with their neighbors and then pray for one another. In silence, each person may reflect and remember, as quiet music is played and video images of Christ touching the lost and lonely are displayed. Or people may jot down a moment of despair, a prayer need, or a cry of anguish on note cards or quilt squares, then bring them forward to pin onto a chain of cards with clothespins on a clothesline, or into a quilt to be stitched and quilted by a sewing team.)

THANKSGIVING AND COMMUNION

Invitation to the Offering (Genesis 21, Psalm 86)

As we bring our needs and our prayers, we also bring our gifts and our service to God. All of these are offerings, placed in trust as we strive to partner with God. Bring your offerings this day, but bring also your anguish and your needs. For in all of these things, God is with us. God can act. God will work through us and with us.

Offering Prayer (Psalm 86)
God of mighty miracles,
> transform these gifts into great works of love
>> and wondrous acts of ministry and grace.

In your holy name, we pray. Amen.

Invitation to Communion (Genesis 21)
Open your eyes, for here is the water of life.
Open your lives, for here is the bread of hope.
Come out of the wilderness of despair
> and sit at the table of promise,
>> for all are welcome here.

SENDING FORTH

Benediction (Genesis 21)
Go forth as signs of hope for a world in despair.
Be love for all you meet!

—OR—

Benediction (Genesis 21)
Though we have been cast aside,
> **God restores our future.**

Though others seek to banish us from sight,
> **God blesses us with opportunities for new life.**

Go with the blessings of the One who loves us fiercely.
> **Amen.**

(B. J. Beu)

CONTEMPORARY OPTIONS

Gathering Words (Genesis 21, Psalm 86)
(Bolded responses are optional if used as a litany. This may also be printed as words for reflection in the program prior to the worship order.)

Sarah sends Hagar into exile.
Hagar gives up on God.
  But God never gives up on Hagar.
God's people are not always good.
  But God never gives up on us.
  For God is with us still.
Even in imperfect people, God's work is done.
Sarah births Isaac.
Hagar and her son birth a great nation for God.
  For God is with us still.
Even in imperfect people, God's work is done.
We learn and grow as children of God.
We help others in spite of our selfishness,
and change lives even without knowing it.
  For God is with us still.

Praise Sentences (Psalm 86)
Lift up your soul, for God is here.
  Praise our great and wondrous God.
Lift up your soul, for God is here.
  Praise our great and wondrous God.

JUNE 29, 2014

Third Sunday after Pentecost, Proper 8
Mary Petrina Boyd

COLOR
Green

SCRIPTURE READINGS
Genesis 22:1-14; Psalm 13; Romans 6:12-23;
Matthew 10:40-42

THEME IDEAS
Today's scriptures speak of trust in God, even in difficult
times. In Genesis, Abraham sets out to accomplish an impossible, agonizing task, only to find that God's love has
gone before him to provide all that he needs. Psalm 13
speaks of struggle, where God seems hidden; yet even
then, the psalmist understands that God's love is steadfast and that life will return with joy. The epistle proclaims
freedom from sin and abundant life in Jesus Christ. The
Gospel encourages people to welcome others as God has
welcomed us. In all these God provides: a ram for the sacrifice, steadfast love to those who despair, righteousness
instead of sin, and a welcome for all people.

INVITATION AND GATHERING

Call to Worship (Psalm 13, Matthew 10)
Come, everyone, come and worship!
God welcomes us all.

Come, all whose hearts are heavy.
God welcomes us all.
Come, all who doubt.
God welcomes us all.
Come, all who trust in God.
God welcomes us all.
Come, everyone, come and worship!

Opening Prayer (Genesis 22, Psalm 13, Matthew 10)
God of love, we come to you as we are.
In the midst of our doubts, our confusion, our failures,
we come with our hopes and our dreams,
trusting that you will provide all that we need
out of your abundant love.
Open our hearts to the richness of your grace,
open our lives to the balm of your mercy,
that we might grow into your community
of life and love. Amen.

PROCLAMATION AND RESPONSE

Prayer of Confession (Genesis 22, Psalm 13, Matthew 10)
Merciful God,
we are reluctant to admit our unfaithful ways:
we have not trusted you completely;
we have ignored those who thirst for your grace;
we have not welcomed others with your love.
Free us from all that keeps us enslaved to sin and death.
Teach us to walk in the ways
of your righteousness,
that we may leave the shadows of darkness
and move into the light
of your steadfast love. Amen.

Words of Assurance (Romans 6)
Sin has no power over you,
for by God's abundant grace,
we are forgiven and set free
to live in joy and love.

Passing the Peace of Christ (Matthew 10:40 NRSV)

Jesus said, "Whoever welcomes you welcomes me, and whoever welcomes me welcomes the one who sent me." Let us welcome one another with the love of God.

Prayer of Preparation (Psalm 13, Matthew 10)

We come to you, O God,
    with fears and doubts.
Open our hearts,
    that we might welcome your word
        of love and abundance. Amen.

Response to the Word (Genesis 22, Psalm 13, Romans 6, Matthew 10)

We thirst for your presence, O God.
Come and be living water in our lives.
When we feel that you have forgotten us,
    draw close to us
        and remind us of your steadfast love.
When things feel difficult,
    show us that you are with us
        and provide for our needs.
When we are tempted,
    assure us of the freedom of life in Christ.
When we feel estranged from you,
    welcome us with your grace,
        that your love may transform us
            in the arms of your mercy. Amen.

—OR—

Response to the Word (Genesis 22, Psalm 13, Romans 6, Matthew 10)

When the knife is raised...
    God stays the hand.
When the heart despairs...
    God's love is steadfast.
When darkness clouds our sight
    God gives light to our eyes.
When we feel dead...

God offers us eternal life.
When people reject us . . .
God welcomes us home.

THANKSGIVING AND COMMUNION

Invitation to the Offering (Matthew 10)

Jesus told his disciples that in giving to others they would find their reward. Let our offerings provide cold water to the thirsty and welcome to the stranger. Let us rejoice as we offer our gifts.

Offering Prayer (Genesis 22, Psalm 13, Matthew 10)

God of love, you provide everything we need
    and deal bountifully with us.
Our hearts rejoice in your love.
We praise you as we share our gifts,
    in the prayer that our offering
        may bring your blessings of living water
            to a thirsty world. Amen.

Invitation to Communion (Psalm 13, Romans 6, Matthew 10)

The God of abundant grace calls us to the Lord's table, where all are welcome. Here, we drink from the cup of forgiveness, which quenches our deepest thirst. Here, we eat from the bread of life, which feeds us with God's steadfast love. God provides abundantly for everyone. Come and rejoice in God!

SENDING FORTH

Benediction

Go forth to welcome the world with the love of God.
Offer water to those who thirst,
    hope to those who despair,
    and life to those who know only death.
Go in God's steadfast love.
May the blessing of God's abundant care
    bring you peace.

CONTEMPORARY OPTIONS

Gathering Words (Psalm 13, Romans 6, Matthew 10)
(Consider having different voices read the light print.)
I come with doubts.
You are God's child and are welcome here.
I'm not very important.
You are God's child and are welcome here.
I'm not good enough.
You are God's child and are welcome here.
I'm not very popular.
You are God's child and are welcome here.
I want to know God.
You are God's child and are welcome here.

Praise Sentences (Psalm 13, Matthew 10)
Sing to the Lord!
God provides for us!
Sing and rejoice, for God is good!
God welcomes us all!

Contemporary Response to the Word
(Echoes the South African song "Freedom Is Coming")
Sin has no power.
Freedom is coming!
Death is no more.
O yes, I know!
Wickedness is gone.
Freedom is coming!
We have eternal life.
O yes, I know!

JULY 6, 2014

Fourth Sunday after Pentecost,
Proper 9
_____
Deborah Sokolove

COLOR
Green

SCRIPTURE READINGS
Genesis 24:34-38, 42-49, 58-67; Psalm 45:10-17; Romans 7:15-25a; Matthew 11:16-19, 25-30

THEME IDEAS
Rebekah's example of gracious generosity is a reflection of the abundant grace of God, but like Paul, we often wrestle with ourselves, giving in to selfish urges instead of doing what we know is right. Jesus invites us to exchange this heavy burden for his light yoke and find rest in him.

INVITATION AND GATHERING

Call to Worship (Romans 7, Psalm 45, Matthew 11)
The Holy One calls us to delight in God's ways.
    We come with our anxiety, our fears, our sorrows.
The Holy One offers us an easy yoke.
    We come yearning to lay our burdens down.
The Holy One promises rest for our souls.
    With joy and gladness, we enter God's house.
    We will praise God's holy name forever and ever.

Opening Prayer (Genesis 24, Matthew 11)

Holy, generous source of all abundance,
    when Abraham's servant came to the spring,
        thirsty and covered with dust from the trail,
            Rebekah offered him more than he asked for,
                giving water to his camels, also.
Today, we come to this place, looking for rest,
    thirsty for the waters of life.
Fill our dry, dusty hearts,
    until they overflow into the world around us
        like rivers of joy and peace. Amen.

PROCLAMATION AND RESPONSE

Prayer of Confession (Romans 7, Matthew 11)

We do not understand our own actions.
    We do not do what we want,
    but the very thing we hate.
We do not do the good we want,
but the evil we do not want to do.
    We delight in the ways of God
    in our inmost selves,
    yet our lives are captive
    to the ways of sin.
Holy One, forgive our inability
to live according to your will.
    Free us to live in peace
    with one another, and with you.

Words of Assurance (Matthew 11)

The Holy One offers us an easy yoke, a light burden,
and rest.
In the name of Christ, you are forgiven.
    In the name of Christ, you are forgiven.
    Glory to God. Amen.

—OR—

170

Prayer of Confession (Romans 7, Matthew 11)
Merciful God, we do not understand our own actions—
we do not do the things we want,
but the very things we detest.
Forgive our foolish ways.
Reclaim us as children of your promise.
Give us the strength and the courage
to bear your yoke willingly,
and heed your call faithfully.
In Christ's name, we pray. Amen.

(Mary J. Scifres)

Words of Assurance (Romans 7, Matthew 11)
Who will rescue us from our foolish ways
and misguided acts?
Only Christ, who is gentle and humble of heart.
In Christ, God's yoke is made easier,
God's burden lighter.
For in Christ, we are made perfect,
even in our imperfection.
Thanks be to God!

(Mary J. Scifres)

Passing the Peace of Christ (Matthew 11)
Lay down your heavy burdens, and live in peace with one another.
The peace of Christ be with you.
The peace of Christ be with you always.

Response to the Word (Genesis 24, Matthew 11)
Bearing the yoke of Christ,
we are called to bring the water of life
to all who thirst.

THANKSGIVING AND COMMUNION

Invitation to the Offering (Matthew 11)
Let us bring our gifts and offerings to the One who offers us rest.

Offering Prayer
Holy, generous Giver of all that is good,
add our small gifts to the everflowing spring
of your love.
Use them to satisfy the thirst
of a world yearning for your waters of life.

Great Thanksgiving
Christ be with you.
And also with you.
Lift up your hearts.
We lift them up to God
Let us give our thanks to the Holy One.
It is right to give our thanks and praise.

It is a right, good, and joyful thing,
always and everywhere, to give you our thanks.
You have made your ways known to us
by the example of your children throughout the ages.
We give you thanks for your daughter, Rebekah,
whose generosity to Abraham's servant
gave witness to her calling
as a mother of your people.

And so, with your creatures on earth
and all the heavenly chorus,
we praise your name, and join their unending hymn:
Holy, holy, holy Lord, God of power and might,
heaven and earth are full of your glory.
Hosanna in the highest. Blessed is the one
who comes in the name of the Lord.
Hosanna in the highest.

Holy are you, and holy is your child, Jesus Christ,
who makes our burdens light
and teaches us to delight in you.
On the night before his death, Jesus took bread,
gave thanks to you, broke the bread,

and gave it to the disciples, saying:
"Take, eat; this is my body which is given for you.
Do this in remembrance of me."
When the supper was over, Jesus took the cup,
offered thanks, and gave it to the disciples, saying:
"Drink from this, all of you;
this is my life in the new covenant,
poured out for you and for many,
for the forgiveness of sins.
Do this, as often as you drink it,
in remembrance of me."
And so, in remembrance of your mighty acts
in Jesus Christ, we proclaim the mystery of faith.
Christ has died.
Christ is risen.
Christ will come again.

Pour out your Holy Spirit on us gathered here,
and on these gifts of bread and wine.
Make them be for us the body and blood of Christ,
that we may be the body of Christ
to a broken, thirsty world.
Easer of burdens, Water for the thirsty, Giver of rest,
we praise your holy, eternal name.
Amen.

SENDING FORTH

Benediction
Take on the easy yoke of Christ.
Carry the water of life to a thirsty world
and you will find rest for your souls.
Amen.

CONTEMPORARY OPTIONS

Gathering Words (Psalm 45)
The Holy One promises rest for our souls.

With joy and gladness we enter the house of God.

—*OR*—

Gathering Words

Are we a generation of complainers, cynics,
and critics?
Rescue us for lives of joyful discipleship!
Are we a people who refuse to dance
when Christ plays?
Rescue us for lives of joyful discipleship!
Are we a people hardened by the world's woes,
who neglect to mourn for those in despair?
Rescue us for lives of joyful discipleship!
Are we a people afraid to follow where God leads?
Rescue us for lives of joyful discipleship!
Christ has rescued us from negative thoughts,
freeing us for lives of joyful living.
**Thanks be to God! Let us praise Jesus Christ,
and answer God's call!**

(Mary J. Scifres)

Praise Sentences (Psalm 45)

Easer of burdens, Water for the thirsty, Giver of rest,
we praise your Holy Name forever and ever.

—*OR*—

Praise Sentences (Psalm 45)

Let's celebrate God's love every day!
Praise God forever and ever!
Let's celebrate God's love every day!
Praise God forever and ever!

(Mary J. Scifres)

JULY 13, 2014

Fifth Sunday after Pentecost, Proper 10
B. J. Beu

COLOR
Green

SCRIPTURE READINGS
Genesis 25:19-34; Psalm 119:105-112; Romans 8:1-11; Matthew 13:1-9, 18-23

THEME IDEAS
God is the sower, we are the seed. Matthew's parable of the Sower mirrors the reality of our world. The word of God simply does not seem to take root in some people; or if it does, it quickly burns out. And despite God's life-giving precepts and teachings, some people choose to follow their baser instincts, which Paul calls "lives based on selfishness" (v. 5). In the church, we believe that the soil of our lives can change. The cares of the world sometimes choke the word that people hear, but it need not be so forever. Yet, it always seems to be a struggle—a struggle reflected in our Genesis reading. Rebekah's children struggle within her. Two parents struggle to love their children, yet each has a favorite. Two brothers struggle to find their place in God's world as they answer God's call. Today's scriptures reflect these struggles, even as they offer a lamp to our feet and light for our journey as we grow in the Spirit.

INVITATION AND GATHERING

Call to Worship (Matthew 13)
You are the Sower, O God; we are the seed.
God's word is being sown in our lives this day.
In God, we live and move and have our being.
You are the Lover, O God; we are the beloved.
God's love blossoms in our lives
with a beauty greater than the lilies of the field.
You are the Healer, O God; we are the healed.
God's healing flows through our veins
with every beat of our heart.
You are the Potter, O God; we are the clay.
God's hand fashions us into lamps
to shine forth the light of Christ.
Come! Let us worship the One
who sows us in the fields of Love.

Opening Prayer (Matthew 13)
Great Sower,
     cast us like seeds upon the winds of your mercy,
          that we may grow in fertile ground.
Keep our lives from stony pathways,
     where the heat of life's cares and strife
          might strip us of our strength and vitality.
Protect us from the thorny gullies,
     where the snares of life's worries and fears
          might choke off our opportunity
               to reach the sunshine of your Spirit.
Land us safely in rich soil, Master Gardener,
     and bless us with the kiss of gentle rain,
          that our faith may increase
               and our joy may be complete. Amen.

PROCLAMATION AND RESPONSE

Prayer of Confession (Matthew 13, Romans 8, Psalm 119)
Caretaker of our souls,
     strengthen our spirit

to resist the allures of prestige and status,
　　that we might not pierce ourselves
　　　　with the arrows of earthly passion.
Grant us the confidence
　　to bloom where we are planted,
　　　　that righteousness and peace
　　　　　　might flower in our lives.
Forgive our fear of appearing foolish
　　in the eyes of others,
　　　　as we experience new growth in your Spirit.
Nurture us with your grace and mercy,
　　and lead us from paths of death and destruction,
　　　　that we might blossom and bloom
　　　　　　as followers of Christ. Amen.

Words of Assurance (Romans 8, Matthew 13)
Those who abide in the Spirit have been set free.
Those who are in Christ find no condemnation.
As forgiven people made new in God's Spirit,
　　rejoice in the fertile ground
　　　　of God's love and mercy.

Introduction to the Word
Do not give up on us, O God,
　　for we are here to follow your precepts
　　　　and return to your ways.
Speak to us again of your ways of life and death,
　　that we may grow strong in our faith
　　　　and bear the fruit of eternal life. Amen.

Response to the Word (Psalm 119)
Your word is a lamp to our feet, O God.
　　Your instructions are a light to our path.
Your decrees are a living heritage.
　　Your teaching is a blessing in times of trial.
Hold our hands and guide us, Holy One.
　　May we abide in your ways and live.

Call to Prayer (Psalm 119)
The wicked lay snares for us,
　　but in God we dwell secure.

The shadows of life threaten us,
    but God is a lamp to our feet
        and a light to our path.
Come, let us offer our prayers to God,
    the One who brings joy to our hearts
        and healing to our wounds.
Let us pray together.
(Invite the congregation to offer prayers of petition and thanks-
giving, followed by a period of silence.)

THANKSGIVING AND COMMUNION

Invitation to the Offering (Matthew 13)
Like a field ready for harvest,
    our lives bear the marks
        of God's love and care.
May we, who bear the fruit of God's labor,
    rejoice as people who have been blessed.
Remembering those who are in want,
    let us bring our tithes and our offerings
        with love and thanksgiving this day.

Offering Prayer (Matthew 13)
Master Gardener,
    as you have sown our lives in rich, fertile soil,
        may we bear much fruit through our giving.
With these offerings,
    may we help bring your realm here on earth,
        as we plant seeds of hope in the fields of life.
Bless our efforts and nourish our efforts,
    that together, we may reap a harvest
        of generosity and love. Amen.

SENDING FORTH

Benediction (Psalm 119, Matthew 13)
God's word is a lamp to our feet.
    Christ's teachings are a light to our path.
May God's word be planted with loving hands
and take root in our lives.

May Christ's edicts nourish us,
like the sunshine and the rain,
and help us grow strong and secure.
God's word is a lamp to our feet.
Christ's teachings are a light to our path.

CONTEMPORARY OPTIONS

Gathering Words (Matthew 13)
We are like seeds on the wind,
set free by the Sower.
Save us, hand of God,
from the rocky pathways
and the thorny ground.
In Christ, we find good soil.
Holy One, may we grow as we should.
Come! Let us worship the Sower,
who plants us in the fields of life.

Praise Sentences (Psalm 119)
God is our lamp.
God is our light.
God's word brings life.
Christ's word brings life.
God is our lamp.
God is our light.

JULY 20, 2014

Sixth Sunday after Pentecost, Proper 11

B. J. Beu

COLOR

Green

SCRIPTURE READINGS

Genesis 28:10-19a; Psalm 139:1-12, 23-24; Romans 8:12-25; Matthew 13:24-30, 36-43

THEME IDEAS

The theme of God's searching love unfolds and deepens with each successive scripture reading. As he sleeps, Jacob dreams of a ladder rising to heaven with angels of the Lord ascending and descending upon it. The psalmist proclaims that God pursues us everywhere, from the farthest reaches of the sea to the very depths of Sheol. Paul urges us to give thanks for life in the Spirit by living as children of God rather than as children of the flesh. Jesus tells his disciples the parable of the wheat and the tares to remind them that though children of darkness surround us, our task is to focus on living as children of light. God's salvific love does not just appear in one spot of hallowed ground in the desert, it pursues us every minute of every day. God's searching love heals us (and all creation), making us children of adoption, children of the Most High. Our proper response to such love is deep gratitude, not hostility to those who have not yet found their way.

INVITATION AND GATHERING

Call to Worship *(Genesis 28, Psalm 139)*
This is none other than the house of God.
This is no less than the gate of heaven.
Surely the presence of the Lord is in this place.
God hems us in, behind and before,
and lays hands of blessing upon us.
Such knowledge is too wonderful to imagine.
It is so high we cannot attain it.
Rejoice, for we are in the house of God.
Give thanks and sing, for this is the gate of heaven.
Surely the presence of the Lord is in this place.

Opening Prayer *(Genesis 28, Psalm 139)*
Great explorer,
    you have searched us and known us,
        and are acquainted with all our ways;
    you hem us in, behind and before,
        and discern our thoughts from afar;
    you know when we sit down
        and when we rise up;
    you are closer to us than our very breath.
Such knowledge is too wonderful for us,
    it is so high we cannot attain it.
If we take the wings of the morning,
    and settle at the farthest limits of the sea,
        even there your hand shall lead us,
            and your might shall hold us fast.
Search us, O God, in this time of worship
    and test the measure of our hearts.
Breathe your Spirit within us,
    and claim us as children of light,
        that everyone we meet might be blessed
            through the gift of your Spirit. Amen.

PROCLAMATION AND RESPONSE

Prayer of Confession (Romans 8, Matthew 13)

Holy Mystery, it is easier to hear the groans of creation
and the cries of the earth
in the devastation of the rain forests,
than it is to hear the groans of our own spirit
and the loss of our own dignity;
it is easier to spot the weeds that grow
in the lives of our adversaries
as they tear the fabric of love asunder,
than it is to see the same weeds that grow
within ourselves as we fall back in worry,
and become slaves to our fear.
You have not given us a spirit of slavery
to fall back into our fear,
but rather a spirit of adoption
as children of God.
Yet the hurts we nurse within
often keep our hearts in bondage
and prevent us from claiming our true freedom
in Christ Jesus.
Release us, Holy One, from the chains that bind us,
that we may be a people of hope once more.
Release us, Great Spirit,
that we may be truly free. Amen.

Words of Assurance (Romans 8:15b-17a)

Hear the words of the Apostle Paul:
"With this Spirit, we cry, 'Abba, Father.' The same Spirit
agrees with our spirit, that we are God's children. But
if we are children, we are also heirs. We are God's heirs
and fellow heirs with Christ."
As children of the living God,
know that you are forgiven and free.

Passing the Peace of Christ (Romans 8)

As children adopted into the family of God, greet one another as fellow children of light by passing the peace of
Christ.

Response to the Word (Psalm 139)

Search us and know us, O God.
Test our hearts and know our thoughts.
See if there is any wickedness
    that clings to us like dew to the grass.
Search us and know us, O God.
Lead us in the way of everlasting life.

—OR—

Response to the Word (Matthew 13)

God of abundance,
    you cause the sun to shine
        on the righteous and the unrighteous;
    you cause the rain to fall
        on the just and the unjust.
Teach us the wisdom
    to allow the weeds to grow alongside the wheat,
        that we don't uproot the good
            in our attempt to be rid of the evils
            in our world. Amen.

THANKSGIVING AND COMMUNION

Ofering Prayer (Genesis 28)

God of dreams and visions,
    open our eyes to see your angels
        ascending to heaven and descending to earth
            as they bring your manifold blessings;
    open our hearts to offer you our thanks and praise
        as we pour out the oil of gladness
        in honor and witness
            of your presence among us.
May the gifts we bring this day
    be signs of our gratitude for your love
        and our commitment to be a blessing
            to all the peoples of mother earth. Amen.

SENDING FORTH

Benediction (Genesis 28, Psalm 139, Matthew 13)
Wherever you are on life's journey,
open your eyes to see the gate of heaven.
The wings of the morning
bring us the presence of God.
Wherever you are on the highway of life,
honor and respect the weeds that grow
among the wheat.
The farthest reaches of the sea
are alive with God's Spirit.
Wherever you are in the seasons of life,
take time to mark holy encounters
with the oil of gladness.
Our hearts are ablaze with God's holy fire.
Go as children of the living God.

CONTEMPORARY OPTIONS

Gathering Words (Psalm 139)
If we take the wings of the morning,
God soars with us.
If we go to the farthest limits of the sea,
God sails with us there.
If we journey to the highest heaven,
God travels with us.
If we sink into the deepest darkness,
God lights our way.
Come! Let us take the wings of the morning
and learn to fly with the One
who is the wind beneath our wings.

Praise Sentences (Genesis 28)
Surely the presence of the Lord is in this place.
God is with us here.
Surely this is the gate of heaven.
God is with us now.
Surely the presence of the Lord is in this place.
God is with us always.

JULY 27, 2014

Seventh Sunday after Pentecost, Proper 12

B. J. Beu

COLOR

Green

SCRIPTURE READINGS

Genesis 29:15-28; Psalm 105:1-11, 45b; Romans 8:26-39; Matthew 13:31-33, 44-52

THEME IDEAS

Good things come to those who wait. Or as Paul would put it: "We know that God works all things together for good for the ones who love God, for those who are called according to [God's] purpose" (8:28). Today's scriptures encourage us to trust that God's realm is worth waiting for. Laban tricks Jacob into marrying Leah rather than Rachel, but without this first marriage, we would not have ten of the twelve tribes of Israel. The psalmist extols God for the blessing of the covenant made with Abraham and his descendents. Paul expresses the conviction that nothing can separate us from the love of God in Christ Jesus. Finally, if we pursue the kingdom of God, and treat it as a gift of great value, we will have joy. Truly, all things do work together for those who love God!

INVITATION AND GATHERING

Call to Worship (Psalm 105, Romans 8)
> Give thanks to the Lord and sing God's praise.
> **Make known God's deeds among the people.**
> Seek the Lord and trust God's strength.
> **Proclaim God's wonderful works far and wide.**
> Let those who seek the Lord rejoice.
> **Let all people extol God's grace.**
> Give thanks to the Lord and sing God's praise.
> **Make known God's deeds among the people.**

Opening Prayer (Matthew 13)
> Glorious God, your kingdom is like a mustard seed
>   that grows into a great shrub
>   where the birds of the air
>   can build their nests;
>   your kingdom is like a treasure hidden in a field,
>   or a pearl of great value.
> Train our hearts to desire your kingdom, Holy One,
>   more than the lesser values of this world.
> Train our eyes to see through the fog
>   that clouds our vision
>   and prevents us from seeing the glory
>   of your realm here on earth.
> May our spirit be uneasy
>   until we have forsaken all that binds us
>   and all that keeps us from building your kingdom
>   in our communities and in our world. Amen.

PROCLAMATION AND RESPONSE

*Prayer of Confession (Genesis 29, Psalm 105,
Romans 8, Matthew 13)*
> Eternal God, it isn't easy to be a people of waiting:
>   waiting for justice,
>   waiting for peace,
>   waiting for love,
>   waiting for your realm

to be established here on earth.
We read of Jacob's willingness to work fourteen years
    for the right to marry the woman he loves,
    but such commitment seems beyond us.
We hear of Abraham's patience
  as he waited for your promises to be fulfilled,
    and we admit to ourselves
      that we would have given up
        long before the end.
Remind us again, God of the ages,
  that all things work together for good
    for those who love you and who are called
      according to your purposes.
Strengthen our faith,
  that our waiting may be transformed
    into hope and action
      for the building of your kingdom
        here on earth. Amen.

Words of Assurance (Romans 8:38-39)

Nothing can separate us from the love of God:
  Not death, nor life, nor angels, nor rulers,
  nor things present, nor things to come.
No power on heaven or under the earth
can separate us from the love of Christ:
  Not height, nor depth,
  nor anything else in all creation.
  Thanks be to God!

Response to the Word (Psalm 105)

Look around, God's judgments are in the earth.
  They are in the waters we drink,
  the waters that claim us in our baptism.
They are in the sky above,
in the rainbow that paints the horizon
after a summer rain.
  God is mindful of us and is faithful
  to the covenants God has made.

Even to a thousand generations God is faithful.
Give thanks to the Lord, you people of God.
May God's praises be always on our lips.

Call to Prayer (Romans 8, Matthew 13)

Spirit of God, when life becomes more than we can bear,
    you intercede for us
        with sighs too deep for words;
    when our need exceeds the hope that is within us,
        you shore up our sagging spirit
            and lift our sight to see new heights.
As we gather in prayer this day,
    set our hearts and minds on you, Holy Spirit,
        that we may know the peace that passes
            all understanding.
As we raise our petitions and praise to your gates,
    plant within us the faith that springs forth
        into newness of life and rededication of purpose,
            that we may be children of your Spirit
                and of Christ's gracious love. Amen.

THANKSGIVING AND COMMUNION

Invitation to the Offering (Romans 8, Matthew 13)

All things work together for good for those who love God, and are called according to God's purposes. Let us approach God's kingdom as a treasure hidden in a field, joyfully selling all we have to buy this field. Let us see God's kingdom as a pearl of great value, gratefully trading our worldly possessions for this one great prize. Let us give back to God, as those who are offered God's very kingdom.

Offering Prayer (Psalm 105, Matthew 13)

Giver of all good gifts,
    your blessings of love and life
        fill our world with hope for the future.
For the lesson of patient waiting,
    we give you thanks.

For the opportunity to bring your realm here on earth,
  we give you praise.
Bless the gifts we lay before you this day,
  that they may be bricks and mortar
    to build your kingdom
      in a world waiting to be remade. Amen.

Communion Prayer (Matthew 13)
Bakerwoman God,
  bless this gift of bread
    with the yeast of your love.
Flow through this gift of wine
  with your life-giving grace.
As we receive these gifts,
  make us one with you
    through the power of your Holy Spirit.
Nurture our lives,
  that we may be loaves
    of your generous abundance.
Pour your grace into our hearts,
  that we may be vines of loving nourishment
    for one another and for a world in need
      of growth and strength.
In Christ's name, we pray. Amen.

(Mary J. Scifres)

SENDING FORTH

Benediction (Matthew 13, Romans 8)
Like a treasure hidden in a field,
God offers us the kingdom.
  **All things work together for good
  for those who love God.**
Like a pearl of great value,
God offers us the kingdom.
  **All things work together for good
  for those who follow Christ.**
Like a mustard seed that grows into a great shrub,
God offers us the kingdom.

All things work together for good
for those who abide in God's Spirit.

—OR—

Benediction (Romans 8:29-30)
Hear these words from the Apostle Paul.
  Those whom God has chosen
    are predestined to be conformed
    to the image of Christ.
  And those predestined to be conformed
    to the image of Christ are also called.
  All those who are called are also justified.
  And all those God justifies, God also glorifies.
Go with the blessings of Almighty God.

CONTEMPORARY OPTIONS

Gathering Words (Matthew 13)
A field filled with treasure...
  the realm of God is beyond price.
Yeast that makes bread to rise...
  the realm of God brings life.
A pearl of unsurpassed beauty...
  the realm of God is worth a lifetime of waiting.
A net that catches all the fish of the sea...
  the realm of God catches us all.
Come! Let us worship the One
who offers us the kingdom.

Praise Sentences (Psalm 105)
Praise the Lord!
  Sing praises to God's name.
Praise the Lord!
  Give thanks to God.
Praise the Lord!
  Praise the Lord!
Praise the Lord!

AUGUST 3, 2014

Eighth Sunday after Pentecost, Proper 13
B. J. Beu

COLOR

Green

SCRIPTURE READINGS

Genesis 32:22-31; Psalm 17:1-7, 15; Romans 9:1-5; Matthew 14:13-21

THEME IDEAS

Doubt, faith, and blessing are interwoven in today's scripture readings. Jacob doubts he can cross Esau's land without being attacked, so he sends his family and flocks ahead. When confronted by an angel, Jacob is not shamed by his earlier lack of faith, but demands to be blessed. Paul has no doubt that God has called him to preach to the Gentiles, yet this does not annul the blessings God has bestowed upon Israel. And while Jesus' disciples want to send the crowds away for food, Jesus knows that they could bless the hungry followers with food if they had sufficient faith. Even in our doubts, blessings are to be had by those who have faith in the One who blesses us. An additional theme is seeing God face to face. Jacob sees God face to face as he struggles with the angel. The psalmist is confident in seeing God's face in righteousness.

INVITATION AND GATHERING

Call to Worship (Psalm 17)

Enter God's gates with lips free of deceit
and tongues free of slander.
We will avoid the ways of the violent,
and keep our feet upon the paths of peace.
Enter God's sanctuary with thanksgiving
and find refuge from the storm.
We come before the Lord with gratitude
to behold God's face in righteousness.
Come! Let us worship the Lord and touch eternity.
We will behold God's likeness and be satisfied.

Opening Prayer (Genesis 32)

Even when our faith falters, O Lord,
we will not let you go.
Even though we are battered and bruised, O God,
we will not let you go.
Because we need your blessing, Holy One,
we will not let you go.
Struggle with us, wrestle with us,
strive with us until the dawn, O Lord,
we will not let you go.
We need your blessing, O God,
and we will not let you go.
Amen.

PROCLAMATION AND RESPONSE

Prayer of Confession (Genesis 32, Matthew 14)

God of mystery and power,
in the midst of our fears and doubts,
you call us home.
Too often, when we are weary,
we lack the courage to take time apart
to regain our strength.
Too often, when our faith wavers,
we seek safety in our own clever schemes.

Too often, when faced with those in need,
   we throw up our hands in defeat,
      sure that there is nothing we can do.
Stay with us when we have need of you, O God,
   and bless us in our struggles,
      that we might be a blessing for others. Amen.

Words of Assurance (Psalm 17, Matthew 14)
Awaken to the good news of God's love:
   In Christ, we are forgiven
   and given strength for the journey.
Rise up and see God face to face
   as you are fed by God's gracious hand.

Passing the Peace of Christ (Psalm 17)
As we strive to keep our feet on the paths of peace, we look to our sisters and brothers in Christ for encouragement and hope for the journey. Let us turn and draw strength from one another as we share signs of Christ's peace.

Response to the Word (Genesis 32, Psalm 17, Matthew 14)
Compassionate One,
   feed us with the wisdom of your word.
Awaken within us
   a longing to see your face,
      that we may be satisfied.
Touch our minds with understanding,
   that we may sense your presence
      in the struggles and wounds of life. Amen.

THANKSGIVING AND COMMUNION

Invitation to the Offering (Matthew 14)
Faced with a hungry crowd and only five loaves and two fish, Jesus fed the multitude until all were satisfied. Faced with a hungry world, God invites us to offer our gifts, that God's bounty may be shared with those in need. May

Christ see our faith and multiply our gifts, that all might
be satisfied.

Offering Prayer (Matthew 14)

Source of Compassion,
all that you have given us is yours.
May our gifts become loaves and fish
for those who are hungry.
May our offerings become love and light
for those who are lost and afraid.
Teach us the joy that comes from sharing our abundance
with those who live in want,
that the world may be fed
and made whole again. Amen.

Invitation to Communion (Matthew 14)

God of our hopes and dreams,
we are empty and long to be filled;
we are hungry and long to be fed;
we are lost and long to be found.
Gather us into your love,
and pick up the pieces of our lives,
just as Jesus gathered up the fragments
of bread and fish
that remained after feeding the crowds.
Call us anew to eat our fill at Christ's table
of the bread of life,
the hope of the ages. Amen.

Communion Prayer (Matthew 14)

Pour out your Holy Spirit on us
and on these gifts of bread and wine.
Make them be for us the life and love of Christ,
that we may be for the world disciples of Christ,
redeemed by your love and fed by your grace.
Awaken us with your Spirit,
that we may be one with Christ,
one with each other,
and one in ministry to the world.

Shine upon our lives,
  that we may we proclaim your love,
    feed the hungry, and show compassion to all,
      until Christ comes in final victory
        and we feast at your heavenly banquet.
Through Jesus the Christ,
  together with the Holy Spirit,
    all honor and glory is yours, Almighty God,
      now and forevermore. Amen.

(Mary J. Scifres)

SENDING FORTH

Benediction (Genesis 32)
  Go forth with the blessing of the One
  who brings you through the wilderness
  into a land flowing with milk and honey.
    We go with the blessings of God,
    who greets us face to face.
  Go with the blessings of the One
  who heals our wounds and makes us whole.
    We go with the blessings of God,
    who bathes us in the power of the Holy Spirit.

CONTEMPORARY OPTIONS

Gathering Words (Matthew 14)
  My people are hungry.
  Give them something to eat.
    There are too many to feed.
  My people are hungry.
  Give them something to eat.
    We have only five loaves and two fish.
  My people are hungry.
  Give them something to eat.
    It would take a miracle.
  With God, all things are possible.
    In Christ, new hope has dawned.

Praise Sentences (Romans 9)

Praise God, who fills us with glory.
Praise God, who joins us in covenant.
Praise God, who adopts us as Christ's family.
Praise God, who writes us into the Book of Life.
Praise God.
Praise God.
Praise God.

—OR—

Praise Sentences (Genesis 32, Matthew 14)

God's love and grace are here!
God's love and grace are here!
Give thanks and endless praise!
Give thanks and endless praise!

(*Mary J. Scifres*)

AUGUST 10, 2014

Ninth Sunday after Pentecost, Proper 14
Mary J. Scifres

COLOR
Green

SCRIPTURE READINGS
Genesis 37:1-4, 12-28; Psalm 105:1-6, 16-22, 45b; Romans 10:5-15; Matthew 14:22-33

THEME IDEAS
The gift of faith saves us—even in times of doubt and struggle, even when that faith is not our own. In our Hebrew Scripture reading, Joseph will one day save his brothers, even though they sold him into slavery in a foreign land. In the Gospel reading, Jesus saved Peter as Peter began to sink. The epistle portrays faith as a beautiful gift that we can offer others when we share the message of Christ's love and grace. Whether we are called out of the boat of doubt or we are calling others out of the boat in a stormy sea, the message of God's constant presence rings true: " 'Be encouraged! It's me. Don't be afraid' " (Matthew 14:27).

INVITATION AND GATHERING

Call to Worship (Psalm 105, Matthew 14)
Come, now is the time to worship.
Now is the time to spring forth in faith.

Give thanks to our God.
   Sing of God's praise and glory.
Seek the Lord.
   Rejoice in God's presence.
Come, now is the time to worship.

Opening Prayer (Genesis 37, Matthew 14)
Steadfast God of faith and grace,
   call to us now.
Carry us out of our fears and doubts
   into the glorious message
      of your saving love
         and constant presence.
Walk with us, O God,
   as we renew our faith,
      discern your call in our lives,
         and journey forth as disciples of Christ. Amen.

PROCLAMATION AND RESPONSE

Call to Confession (Matthew 14)
Take heart! Christ is with us, catching us with grace, even
in our desperate sorrows. Christ is with us, redeeming us
with mercy, even from our deepest sins.

Prayer of Confession (Genesis 37, Psalm 105, Matthew 14)
Faithful One, reach out to us with your grace and mercy.
Forgive us when we sink into sin,
   and when we too easily accept our shortcomings.
Forgive us when we do not venture forth
   when you call us forward in faith.
As we call upon your holy name,
   reclaim us with your mercy and grace,
      that we may be your children—
         forgiven, renewed, and emboldened
            in the greatness of your living faith.

Words of Assurance (Matthew 14)
Take heart! Christ is with us,
    and holds our lives with mercy and grace.
In Christ's love, we are forgiven indeed.

Passing the Peace of Christ (Romans 10)
How beautiful are the feet of those who bring the message of Christ's love. In beauty and joy, let us share that message as we exchange signs of peace and love with one another.

Introduction to the Word (Psalm 105, Romans 10)
Seek God's presence continually—in life, in worship, in the word of God spoken this day. Listen for the message of God's good news.

Response to the Word (Romans 10, Matthew 14)
Walk on the water; live in the struggle.
    We will move forward in faith,
    trusting in God's strength.
Share the good news: Christ is with us.
    The news is beautiful and true:
    Christ calls us forth in mercy and grace.

THANKSGIVING AND COMMUNION

Invitation to the Offering (Psalm 105, Romans 10)
Remembering God's wonderful works, let us share our gifts and offerings, that the message of God's wonderful works and of Christ's saving love may be known throughout the earth.

Offering Prayer (Psalm 105, Romans 10)
Gracious God,
    your gifts are indeed great,
    your works a wonder to behold.
We thank you for the gift
    of your amazing grace,
        as we return a portion of these gifts to you.

Bless these gifts,
  that our giving may become a beautiful message
    of your love and grace.
In Christ's glorious name, we pray. Amen.

Invitation to Communion (Romans 10)

In Christ, there is no east or west. In God's love, there is neither Jew nor Greek. At this table of grace, there is no distinction between stranger and friend, member and visitor, sinner and saint. All are welcome at this feast of love.

SENDING FORTH

Benediction (Romans 10, Matthew 14)

Walk on the water; move forward in faith.
We go forth with the good news of God!

—OR—

Benediction (Psalm 105, Matthew 14)

God blesses us with strength for the journey.
  Our hearts sing God's praises.
Christ lifts us up from the raging waters of life.
  Our spirits rejoice in our salvation.
The Spirit guides us forth
with dreams full of hope and promise.
  Our lives rest secure in the One who is faithful.
Thanks be to God!

(B. J. Beu)

CONTEMPORARY OPTIONS

Gathering Words (Psalm 105, Matthew 14)

(In the response, "our God" may be substituted for "the Lord.")
Seek the Lord, for Christ is present here.
  Come and worship the Lord.
Listen to the Lord, for Christ is calling.
  Come and worship the Lord.
Follow the Lord, for Christ is leading.
  Come and worship the Lord.

Praise Sentences (Psalm 105)
Sing praise to God. Give God glory and praise.
Sing of God's wonderful works!
Sing praise to God. Give God glory and praise.
Sing of God's wonderful works!

AUGUST 17, 2014

Tenth Sunday after Pentecost, Proper 15
B. J. Beu

COLOR
Green

SCRIPTURE READINGS
Genesis 45:1-15; Psalm 133; Romans 11:1-2a, 29-32; Matthew 15:(10-20), 21-28

THEME IDEAS
What unites us is far greater than what divides us, for God creates us to live together in unity. Joseph forgives his brothers for selling him into slavery, for God used this terrible act to save the Israelites and Egyptians alike from famine. The psalmist celebrates when kindred live together in unity. Paul asks rhetorically if God has rejected the Hebrew people by offering salvation to the Gentiles, only to answer, "Absolutely not!" (v. 1). Jesus initially refuses to help a Canaanite woman's daughter until she presses her case. Then Jesus joyfully heals the daughter, marveling at the woman's faith. We are all bound together in the unconditional love of God, and are called to live together in unity.

INVITATION AND GATHERING

Call to Worship (Genesis 45, Psalm 133, Romans 11, Matthew 15)
When hatred and division separate us,
God binds us together in unity.

When past quarrels estrange us from one another,
God binds us together in unity.
When we feel excluded and left out,
God binds us together in unity.
When we forsake others, claiming God is on our side,
God binds us together in unity.
Bind us together, Holy One.
Bind us together in unity.

Opening Prayer (Genesis 45, Psalm 133, Romans 11, Matthew 15)
Holy bond of Love,
    part the veil that keeps us feeling isolated and afraid.
Bind us together in unity.
When our families hurt and betray us,
    help us let go of our pain
        and work for the healing of all.
When we feel abandoned by those we love,
    grant us the ability to forgive
        and to seek peace and reconciliation
            with those who have wronged us.
When our hearts are pierced with anguish,
    teach us to trust once more,
        that we may find solace and grace
            through your loving Spirit. Amen.

PROCLAMATION AND RESPONSE

Prayer of Confession (Genesis 45, Psalm 133, Matthew 15)
Merciful God,
    we envy Joseph for his power to rule Egypt;
    we even admire Joseph
        for recognizing your hand
            in his brother's treachery,
                that life might be preserved
                    in the midst of famine;

but we look at Joseph in awe
when he wept with perfect forgiveness
on the necks of the very brothers
who had sold him into slavery.
Part of your plan or not, gracious One,
we would not be so quick to forgive family
if they had sold us into bondage
after contemplating our murder.
We know that our own anger,
however righteous in our eyes
is poisoning our souls
and the lives of those around us.
Help us know the joy of living in unity,
even with those we would rather live without.

Assurance of Pardon (Psalm 133:1, Romans 11:29)

How very good and pleasing it is
when kindred live together in unity.
The gifts and calling of God are irrevocable.
Rejoice in the knowledge of God's saving love.

Response to the Word (Genesis 45, Psalm 133, Romans 11, Matthew 15)

Even in the midst of tragedy and loss,
God is at work, preserving a remnant.
Thanks be to God!
Even in the midst of abandonment and rejection,
God is at work, saving the faithful.
Thanks be to God!
Even in the midst of insult and injury,
God is at work, healing the needy.
Thanks be to God!
God challenges us to look beyond our differences,
to embrace what we have in common,
and to live together in unity.
Thanks be to God!

THANKSGIVING AND COMMUNION

Offering Prayer (Genesis 45)
Bountiful God, when famine threatened the world,
    you blessed Joseph with dreams
        that preserved life in the midst of famine;
when hunger threatens our world,
    you bless us with dreams
        to preserve life in the midst of disaster.
When our dreams are your dreams, Gracious God,
    the world is truly blessed.
Accept these gifts,
    as a pledge to live the dream
        that all may live together in unity. Amen.

SENDING FORTH

Benediction (Genesis 22, Romans 6)
The God of dreams brings us together.
    The God of dreams seals us in love.
The God of love knits us together in unity.
    The God of love heals all divisions.
The God of all people sends us forth together.
    The God of promise brings us home.

CONTEMPORARY OPTIONS

Gathering Words (Psalm 133)
How awesome it is when everyone gets along.
    They'll know we are Christians by our love.
How great it is when everyone lives as God intends.
    They'll know we are Christians by our love.
They'll know we are Christians by our love.
    They'll know we are Christians by our love.

Praise Sentences (Romans 11)
The gifts of the Lord are irrevocable.
    Praise the God of our salvation.

The calling of the Lord is steadfast and true.
Praise the God of our salvation.
Praise the God of our salvation.
Praise the God of our salvation.

AUGUST 24, 2014

Eleventh Sunday after Pentecost, Proper 16

Safiyah Fosua

COLOR

Green

SCRIPTURE READINGS

Exodus 1:8–2:10; Psalm 124; Romans 12:1-8;
Matthew 16:13-20

THEME IDEAS

A relationship exists among the Matthew, Exodus, and
Romans texts. Matthew 16:13-20 contains the historic
question around which the Christian faith gathers, while
Exodus 1:8–2:10 paints a picture of what it means to be
certain about our faith and its practices. Romans 12 reminds us that the Christian response to the mercies of God
is a surrendered life, a life lived as though it were a sacrifice offered to God.

INVITATION AND GATHERING

Call to Worship (Psalm 124)

If it had not been for God, where would we be?
If it were not for God in our lives,
what kind of people would we be now?
Thank God that we are not left to our own devices.
Thank God that we do not walk alone!

We are not alone.
  Our help is in the name of the Lord,
  who made heaven and earth.
Come! Let us worship the God who is our Sustainer,
  our Redeemer, our Creator, and our Friend!

Opening Prayer (Exodus 1–2, Romans 12, Matthew 16)
  God of our yesterdays and our tomorrows,
    nothing is permanent but your love;
    nothing is certain except your presence.
  When the winds of life change,
    and the mountaintop experience gives way
      to the stark reality of the valley,
        remind us that you are with us still.
  If we should be tempted or pressured
    to compromise our beliefs,
      help us to hold fast to your teachings—
        like the midwives in Moses' day—
          even if it might cost us our livelihood
          or life itself.
  Make us so certain of who you are,
    and of your good work in our lives,
      that we may live before others
        as those who truly belong to Christ. Amen.

PROCLAMATION AND RESPONSE

Prayer of Confession (Matthew 16)
  O God, we too often live our Christian lives
    in the shadows.
  Called to be salt and light,
    we have been tasteless and dim.
  Called to profess our faith publicly,
    we have been hidden and silent,
      imperceptible to those around us.
  Called to champion the voiceless,
    we have chosen comfort over controversy.

By choosing to take the path of least offense,
   we have unwittingly offended you,
      and have cheapened our faith
         in the eyes of our neighbors.
For the many ways we have lived in the shadows,
   forgive us, O God.
Grant us courage,
   that we might shine like lights
      in this challenging world. Amen.

Words of Assurance (Psalm 124)
Hear the good news: God loves us
   and delivers us from trouble,
      even trouble of our own making.
God, who hears our prayers,
   forgives us, and gives us the ability
   to renew our lives.
In the name of Jesus Christ, you are forgiven!

Introduction to the Word or Prayer of Preparation (Exodus 1–2)
Open our ears, O God, to hear today's questions
   through the lives of ancient Hebrew midwives:
      To whom do we belong?
      Where is our allegiance?
      Whom do we fear *most*?

Introduction to the Word or Prayer of Preparation (Matthew 16)
Who do you say that Jesus is? This is more than a question for creedal confessions, this is foundational to our faith and our very Christian identity. After two thousand years, the question must still be asked and answered by those who claim to believe: "Who is Jesus?"

Response to the Word (Exodus 1–2)
It does not matter if we see ourselves as powerless or powerful. The midwives, Moses' mother, and Pharaoh's daughter all stumbled into God's perfect plan by defiantly choosing to do what they thought was right in the face of

great danger. May God give us similar courage to pursue good works, even in hostile environments, as we place our complete trust in God.

—OR—

Response to the Word (Romans 12)
Make my life a living sacrifice, O God.
All that I ever thought I did well;
  all that I ever hope to do or be;
    my substance, my influence;
      anything about me that poses as power;
        all these I pour out at your feet,
          as a living sacrifice to you. Amen.

THANKSGIVING AND COMMUNION

Offering Prayer (Romans 12)
Loving God, we thank you for every gift, large and small,
  that has been offered to you today,
    and ask for your blessing upon us.
Receive these gifts, O God.
Receive also the gifts
  of our time and our service,
    as we pursue your great work.
Receive our presence as a testimony to your goodness,
  and bless our acts of loving kindness
    in places that have known only trouble. Amen.

SENDING FORTH

Benediction (Exodus 1–2, Psalm 124)
Go from this place, with the assurance
that God is in control of every situation.
  We go forth remembering God's faithfulness.
  If it had not been for our God,
  where would we be?
Go from this place, encouraged by the stories
of the Hebrew midwives, of Moses' mother,
and even of Pharaoh's daughter.

We go forth with determination
to serve God in all circumstances.
We go to be a living reminder to the world
of the glory of God!

CONTEMPORARY OPTIONS

Gathering Words (Exodus 1–2)

God, teach us the ancient stories
    that show us how to trust you,
        even in difficult circumstances.
Remind us of the many ways
    that you have used both the high and mighty,
        and the humble and least likely,
            to carry out your perfect will.
Remind us that we are together on this journey,
    as we struggle to trust you more. Amen.

Praise Sentences (Psalm 124)

Lift your hands to God
who truly works in mysterious ways.
    We lift our hands to God!
Lift your voices to God
who waits with us in the storm.
    We lift our voices to God!
Lift your hearts to God,
who knows us and loves us.
    We offer our hands,
    our voices, and our hearts
    to God in worship!

AUGUST 31, 2014

Twelfth Sunday after Pentecost, Proper 17

B. J. Beu

COLOR
Green

SCRIPTURE READINGS
Exodus 3:1-15; Psalm 105:1-6, 23-26, 45c; Romans 12:9-21;
Matthew 16:21-28

THEME IDEAS
Knowing when to turn aside can make all the difference in
the world. Moses sees a bush ablaze with fire yet not consumed and turns aside to see. Only then does God call to
Moses from out of the burning bush. The psalmist urges
the people to turn aside from everyday cares and seek the
Lord, the source of strength and miracles, the fountain of
wonder and joy. Paul exhorts the church of Rome to turn
aside feelings of resentment and hate for their adversaries,
and instead repay evil with good to do what is noble in
the sight of all. Jesus rebukes Peter, saying he must turn
aside from worldly considerations to embrace divine
ones. If we are to find our lives, we must lose them. Such
is the turning aside that must take place if we are to stand
on holy ground.

INVITATION AND GATHERING

Call to Worship (Exodus 3, Psalm 105)

Give thanks to the Lord.
Call on God's holy name.
Sing praises to our God.
Tell of God's wonderful works.
Let the hearts of those who seek the Lord rejoice.
Let the faithful glory in the Lord's awesome power.
Shout to our God.
Proclaim God's miracles
and the judgments of God's mouth.
Give thanks to the Lord.
Rejoice that the Lord has given us a land
flowing with milk and honey.
Let everything that draws breath
praise the living God!

Opening Prayer (Exodus 3, Romans 12)

Great I Am,
    you excite our curiosity,
        inviting us to turn aside
            from the ruts we travel in
                to find holy ground;
    you appear to us in a flame of fire,
        teasing open our imagination
            and revealing windows into our world
                we could not conceive of on our own.
Surprise us once more, Living Flame.
Reveal the wonder of our world as it may be—
    a world where love is genuine,
    a world where evil is hated
        and the saints are honored,
    a world where mutual affection abides,
    a world where hospitality is shown to strangers,
    a world where enemies are loved and cared for,
    a world where all may be one. Amen.

PROCLAMATION AND RESPONSE

Prayer of Confession (Exodus 3, Romans 12, Matthew 16)

God of turning and returning,
> we would rather tend our flocks in peace,
>> than confront the powers
>>> that oppress your people;
> we would rather keep silent in the face of suffering,
>> than speak your truth for all to hear;
> we would rather stoke the fires of indignation,
>> than taste the healing waters of forgiveness;
> we would rather protect our friends at all cost,
>> than see your will be done,
>>> if it means those we love will suffer.

Forgive us for setting our minds on human things
> rather than on things of your kingdom.

May we not taste death, Holy One,
> before we live your kingdom into reality,
>> through Christ our Lord. Amen.

Words of Assurance (Exodus 3, Psalm 105)

The God of our ancestors,
> the God of Abraham and Sarah,
> the God of Isaac and Rebekah,
> the God of Jacob and Leah and Rachel,
> is a God of second chances, a God who invites us
> to turn and return to the paths of the living.

In the name of the great I Am
> who brought us out of bondage,
> and in the power of the Son of Man,
> who leads us into life, we are forgiven.

Passing the Peace of Christ (Romans 12)

Live peaceably with all, holding fast to what is good, honoring what is just, and showing mutual affection, even for our adversaries. In the spirit of the Prince of Peace, who leads us into life, let us turn to one another and pass the peace of Christ.

Introduction to the Word (Exodus 3)

Let us turn aside from the worries and cares that keep us locked in prisons of our own making. Let us take off our shoes and listen with awe and wonder to words from the great I Am—the One who invites us to new and wondrous possibilities—for we are sitting on holy ground.

Response to the Word (Exodus 3, Matthew 16:24-26)

Listen well to Jesus' invitation to life in the Spirit:
"All who want to come after me must say no to themselves, take up their cross, and follow me. All who want to save their lives will lose them. But all who lose their lives because of me will find them. Why would people gain the whole world but lose their lives? What will people give in exchange for their lives?"
Let us turn aside from business as usual,
let us alter our course when we see a bush
alive with fire and yet not consumed.
Let us embrace the One whose teachings lead to life.

THANKSGIVING AND COMMUNION

Offering Prayer (Romans 12:13b, 20 NRSV)

God of new beginnings,
we are prepared to give of ourselves
and of our riches
to help those we deem worthy of our gifts.
Yet, you challenge us to so much more, saying:
"Extend hospitality to strangers...
[and] if your enemies are hungry, feed them;
if they are thirsty, give them something to drink."
Such unconditional love is hard for us.
May today's offering be a sign of our commitment
to rise above our selfish nature
and do what is honorable in the sight of all,
that those in need may find solace
and peace. Amen.

SENDING FORTH

Benediction (Exodus 3, Psalm 105)
The God of our ancestors, the One who appeared
to Moses in a burning bush, continues to appear
to us in flames of fire, offering us the chance
of personal transformation and renewal.
**The God of our ancestors, the God of Abraham
and Sarah, the God of Isaac and Rebekah,
the God of Jacob and Leah and Rachel,
the One who led the Hebrew people from bondage
to freedom, continues to lead us today,
redeeming those who suffer injustice
and oppression.**
May the God of redeeming love
turn our hearts of stone into hearts of flesh,
that we may engage our world
with the transforming power of Christ.
**May the God of miracles and strength
bless us with a faith that perseveres,
overcoming evil with good,
and abiding in steadfast love.**

CONTEMPORARY OPTIONS

Gathering Words (Exodus 3, Matthew 16)
Don't just keep going, turn and see.
A bush in flame, burning but not consumed.
Don't just gawk in surprise, approach and hear.
God calls us to a new beginning.
Don't just stand there with your shoes on.
We are standing on holy ground.
Come! Let us worship the great I Am.

Praise Sentences (Psalm 105)
Give thanks to the Lord.
Shout God's mighty deeds from the mountaintop.
Sing of God's glory in the sanctuary.

Tell of God's strength in the marketplace.
Remember God's wondrous works in prayer.
Give thanks to the Lord.
Give thanks and sing.

SEPTEMBER 7, 2014

Thirteenth Sunday after Pentecost, Proper 18
Mary J. Scifres

COLOR
Green

SCRIPTURE READINGS
Exodus 12:1-14; Psalm 149; Romans 13:8-14; Matthew 18:15-20

THEME IDEAS
God's love covered the ancient Israelites with protection as Death passed over them. God's love covers our lives with hope for the future and new possibilities. Paul reminds the church in Rome that love is the true fulfillment of God's law, and that the love of God within us makes it possible for us to love freely and abundantly. Even human reconciliation and forgiveness are possible because God first loves us and comes into our presence when we gather in God's holy name. Sing for joy, even in the midst of sin and sorrow, for God's love is steadfast and faithful, constantly covering our lives.

INVITATION AND GATHERING

Call to Worship (Psalm 149)
Sing a new song to God.
Sing of light and hope.

Praise with dancing and joy.
Praise with lives of love.
Rejoice with strings and drums.
Rejoice with justice and peace.

Opening Prayer (Exodus 12, Romans 13, Matthew 18)

Holy One of ancient times,
    we enter your presence
        to remember and rejoice.
Cover us with your love,
    that we may put on the protection
        of your steadfast faithfulness.
Guide us with your love,
    that we may seek reconciliation
        with true repentance and genuine forgiveness.
Strengthen us with your love,
    that we may pursue justice
        and live compassionate lives.
With gratitude, in remembrance of your mighty gifts,
    we pray. Amen.

PROCLAMATION AND RESPONSE

Prayer of Confession (Exodus 12, Romans 13, Matthew 18)

Gracious God, amidst our songs of joy,
    our hearts are touched by fear.
Sin plagues our world,
    even as we try to hide from the truth
        of our ugliest thoughts and actions.
Sorrow enters our lives,
    even as we put on false smiles
        and engage in empty conversation.
Death comes,
    even as we struggle against the grim reality
        of our own mortality.
Cover us with your forgiveness and grace, Holy One,
    and reconcile us with your love and compassion.

Bring us ever closer to you,
>that we may be gathered in your name,
>>welcomed in your presence,
>>>and filled with the joy
>>>>of your steadfast love and hope.

Words of Assurance (Romans 13, Matthew 18)
Where two or three are gathered in Christ's name,
>God is with us.
Where God is present,
>there is grace and compassion.
Having put on Christ Jesus,
>we are forgiven and reconciled,
>one with Christ, one with each other,
>and one in ministry with the world.

Passing the Peace of Christ (Matthew 18)
Let us loose the bonds of unfamiliarity, anger, and sorrow by offering signs of love, peace, and reconciliation to one another.

Introduction to the Word (Exodus 12)
These words of Scripture are words of remembrance, stories of God's people, words of God's wisdom, hope for the future, and challenge for the present. Listen for the word of God.

Response to the Word or Benediction (Romans 13)
It is time.
>**Time to wake from sleep.**
It is time.
>**Time to lay aside laziness and inattentiveness.**
It is time.
>**Time to look up and see Christ's shining hope.**
It is time.
>**Time to live in the shimmer of God's wisdom.**
It is time.
>**Time to put on love as the clothing of life.**
(If used as a Benediction, add) It is time.
Time to go forth as the people of God!

THANKSGIVING AND COMMUNION

Invitation to the Offering (Exodus 12, Romans 13)

Does God desire burnt offerings or gifts of perfect devotion? In Christ, all gifts are welcome, both great and small. Covered in love, led by compassion, let us share our gifts and offerings with God.

Offering Prayer (Romans 13)

Receive these gifts as offerings of love, O God.
Bless them with your grace,
 that all who receive them
  may be covered in compassion
   and led by hope.
In your holy name, we pray. Amen.

The Great Thanksgiving (Exodus 12, Matthew 18)

The Lord be with you.
And also with you.
Lift up your hearts.
We lift them up to the Lord.
Let us give thanks to the Lord our God.
It is right to give our thanks and praise.

It is right, and a good and joyful thing,
 always and everywhere to give thanks to you,
 almighty God, creator of heaven and earth.
From ancient times, you create us in your image,
 call us to be your people,
 and lead us on the paths of life.
When we were lost and afraid,
 in your compassion and forgiveness
 you passed over us,
 offering a path of new beginnings and hope.
Even when we turned away,
 you continued to walk with us,
 extending the hand of steadfast love.
In the words of the prophets,
 you offered your wisdom and your truth.

And in the fullness of time, you sent your Son,
   Christ Jesus, to reveal your grace in the world,
   and to call us to reconciliation
   and faithful relationship.

And so, with your people on earth,
   and all the company of heaven,
   we praise your name
   and join their unending hymn, saying:
   **Holy, holy, holy Lord, God of power and might,
      heaven and earth are full of your glory.
   Hosanna in the highest. Blessed is the one
      who comes in the name of the Lord.
   Hosanna in the highest.**

Holy are you and blessed is your salvation and grace,
   through Jesus Christ.
Through Christ's patient love and unfailing grace,
   you invite us into your presence,
   rescue us from our sins,
   and lead us in your path of righteousness.
With Christ's presence in our lives,
   you cover us with your grace
   and invite us into fullness of life and love.
In remembrance and gratitude,
   we break this bread remembering the words
   of your Son:
"Take, eat; this is my body which is given for you.
   Do this in remembrance of me."
As we fill this cup, we give thanks
   and remember Jesus' words of life:
"Drink from this, all of you.
This is my life poured out for you, and for many,
   in a new covenant for the forgiveness of sins.
Do this, as often as you drink it, in remembrance of me."

And so, in remembrance of these
   your mighty acts of love and grace,

we offer ourselves in praise and thanksgiving
as a holy and living sacrifice,
in union with Christ's offering for us,
as we proclaim the mystery of faith.
Christ has died.
Christ is risen.
Christ will come again.

Communion Prayer

Pour out your Holy Spirit on our fellowship
and on these gifts of bread and wine,
that we might be filled
with your compassion and love,
and led by your wisdom and truth.
Cover us with your love,
that by your Spirit we might be one with Christ,
one in reconciliation with each other,
and one in the ministry of love to the world
until Christ comes in final victory
and we feast at the heavenly banquet.
Through Jesus Christ,
with the Holy Spirit in your holy Church,
all honor and glory is yours, almighty God,
now and forevermore. Amen.

Giving the Bread and Cup (Exodus 12, John 4)

(The bread and wine are given with these or other words of blessing.)
Manna in the wilderness, bread for the journey,
Christ's life given for you.
The cup of love, the water of eternal life,
Christ's love poured out for you.

SENDING FORTH

Benediction (Exodus 12, Matthew 18)

We have gathered together, and God has been with us.
We go forth to serve, and God goes before us.
Go with the power of God!

CONTEMPORARY OPTIONS

Gathering Words (Exodus 12, Romans 13, Matthew 18)

Light and life call to us now.
We are welcomed as the people of God!
Sorrow flees, and sin cannot bind us.
We are welcomed as the people of God!
Dawn beckons, and the world yearns to hear the good news of hope!
We are welcomed as the people of God!

Praise Sentences (Psalm 149)

Praise God with dancing, drums, and guitars.
Sing to the God of love!
Praise God with laughter, joy, and song.
Sing to the God of love!

SEPTEMBER 14, 2014

Fourteenth Sunday after Pentecost,
Proper 19

Mary J. Scifres

COLOR

Green

SCRIPTURE READINGS

Exodus 14:19-31; 15:1b-11, 20-21; Romans 14:1-12;
Matthew 18:21-35

THEME IDEAS

The forgiveness taught by Jesus is a challenging concept.
The acceptance and inclusion taught by Paul is equally
challenging. Forgiving 77 times? Vegetarians eating next
to carnivores? Forgiving 10,000 talents? Accept those who
break the Sabbath or other rules we hold sacred? Jesus reminds us that if we withhold forgiveness, forgiveness will
be withheld from us. Paul reminds us that when we judge
others, we will be judged by God. Forgiveness and acceptance bind these two scriptures together, even as they
bind a community together. Woven into unity by the gifts
of grace and welcome, a friendship, a family, a church, a
community, and even a world can live as the people of
God. The Exodus readings point to a different vision of
community: people rescued and redeemed from death
and claimed as God's chosen ones. Suggestions specifically related to the Exodus readings can be found in *The*

Abingdon Worship Annual 2008 or upon request from the editors.

INVITATION AND GATHERING

Call to Worship (Romans 14, Matthew 18)
Welcome to you, the weak and the strong.
Christ Jesus welcomes us here.
Welcome to you, sinners and saints.
God's grace embraces us all.
Welcome to you, forgiven and forgiving.
The Spirit binds us in unity and love.

—*OR*—

Call to Worship (Exodus 14–15, Romans 14)
Sing to our God of strength and might.
Sing to our God of grace and hope.
Sing songs of praise, glory, and joy.
Sing songs of grace, hope, and love.
Sing to our God, with songs of praise.
Sing to our God, with songs of grace.

Opening Prayer (Romans 14)
God of love and grace,
bind us together this day.
Even as you have welcomed us,
so may we welcome one another.
Speak to our hearts,
that we may hear your words
and heed your call
to live as a community
of acceptance and love.

PROCLAMATION AND RESPONSE

Prayer of Confession (Romans 14, Matthew 18)
Forgive us seven times, seventy times,
seventy-seven times, O Lord,
even when we neglect to forgive as freely
as you forgive us.

Forgive us with such abundance and grace,
   that our hearts may overflow
      with gratitude and mercy;
   that we may begin to forgive freely
      and accept others gladly,
         as you have forgiven and accepted us.
Welcome us into your arms of love,
   that we may welcome others
      with compassion and care.
In gratitude we pray. Amen.

Words of Assurance (Romans 14, Matthew 18)
Out of pity, God sees our sins
   and forgives our debt.
So we are called to see with pity
   and forgive with compassion.
Come, we are made new in Christ Jesus,
   given new eyes to see and grace to forgive.
In Christ's grace, we are forgiven and freed.

Passing the Peace of Christ (Romans 14)
As we have been welcomed into God's love, let us now share with one another signs of welcome and love.

Introduction to the Word (Romans 14)
Christ calls to us, reminding us that we do not live for ourselves. We do not listen for ourselves. We listen for God's truth, for God's wisdom. Put to death all judgment, and listen for the word of God.

Response to the Word (Romans 14, Matthew 18)
Merciful One,
   guide us with your mercy and grace.
Strengthen those who are weak;
   humble those who are strong.
Live within us,
   that we may be filled
      with your love and compassion.
Work in our lives,
   that we may forgive as we have been forgiven,

that we may welcome as we have been welcomed,
that we may accept and love as abundantly
  as we have been accepted and loved by you.
In your gracious name, we pray. Amen.

THANKSGIVING AND COMMUNION

Offering Prayer (Romans 14)

Welcome these gifts,
  as you have welcomed us, O God.
Grant that those who receive the ministries
  supported by these gifts,
    may know your compassion and infinite love. Amen.

Invitation to Communion (Romans 14)

Come to the table, for all are welcome.
Come to the meal, for all will be fed.
Come into God's presence, for all are forgiven.
Come join in the feast of love.

SENDING FORTH

Benediction (Romans 14, Matthew 18)

Go with God's welcome.
Go with God's grace.
Go forth to love and embrace God's world.

CONTEMPORARY OPTIONS

Gathering Words (Exodus 14–15, Romans 14, Matthew 18)

Sing of grace and mercy, compassion and care.
  Sing of God's triumph of love!
Sing of forgiveness, acceptance, and welcome for all.
  Sing of God's triumph of love!

Praise Sentences (Exodus 14–15, Romans 14, Matthew 18)

Sing to God, of forgiveness and grace.
  Forgiveness and grace!
Sing of God's welcoming love!

SEPTEMBER 21, 2014

Fifteenth Sunday after Pentecost, Proper 20

B. J. Beu

COLOR

Green

SCRIPTURE READINGS

Exodus 16:2-15; Psalm 105:1-6, 37-45; Philippians 1:21-30; Matthew 20:1-16

THEME IDEAS

Although God provides everything we need to live, we always seem to find something to complain about. In Genesis, the whole congregation complains of hunger and how life was better back in Egypt. The psalmist extols God's bountiful response to the people's wilderness complaining: providing quail in the evening, bread of heaven in the morning, and water from a rock. Paul complains, if only a little, about having to remain here on earth when he could be with Christ in heaven. In Matthew, the day laborers who worked a full day complain that they were treated unfairly, since all were paid the same wages, even those who worked only a short time. Yet, God will be God, showering blessings with equity—even when we complain; perhaps, especially when we complain. And that is good news.

INVITATION AND GATHERING

Call to Worship (Psalm 105, Matthew 20)
Give thanks to the Lord.
Call on God's holy name.
Sing praises to our God.
Tell of God's wonderful works.
The Lord brings quail to eat in the evening
and the bread of heaven in the morning.
God causes water to flow from solid rock,
turning dry desert into a river.
Shout to the Lord.
Proclaim the miracles that bless the people with life.
Give thanks to our God.
Let everything that draws breath praise God!

Opening Prayer (Exodus 16, Psalm 105)
Caretaker God,
    as we wander in the wilderness of our lives,
       lead us with your cloud by day
          and with your pillar of fire by night,
             that we may never lose our way.
Bless us with your presence, Holy One,
    that we may know the strength of your hand
       and the tender mercy of your love.
Feed us with your bread from heaven,
    that we may taste your Spirit
       and shout your praises. Amen.

PROCLAMATION AND RESPONSE

Prayer of Confession (Exodus 16, Psalm 105, Matthew 20)
God of infinite patience,
    O how we love to complain:
       the journey is too long,
       we are hungry,
       we are thirsty,
       we are tired and want to go home,

life isn't fair,
this isn't what we signed up for....
You've heard it all before, faithful One;
you'll hear it all again.
Yet, do not forsake us in our grumbling,
but shower us with your blessings of old,
for we are weary of our own complaining
and long to make a fresh start.
Open our lips to sing songs of gratitude
and we will be reborn.
Open our minds to the glories of your love
and we will shine like the sun.
In your holy name, we pray. Amen.

Words of Assurance (Psalm 105:3b)

Heed the words of the psalmist:
"Let the hearts of those who seek the LORD rejoice."
Rejoice, sisters and brothers in Christ.
Rejoice and count your blessings, not your troubles.
Show gratitude in all things and you will find peace.

Passing the Peace of Christ (Matthew 20:16)

Remembering Christ's words that the first will be last and
the last will be first, let us seek the peace and welfare of
those around us as we share signs of God's peace.

Response to the Word (Philippians 1)

Do not be known as people who live to complain. Be
known as people who are worthy of the gospel of Christ.
With gratitude for the past and hope for the future, you
will possess the inheritance prepared for you. For only in
gratitude are we able to embrace the fullness of God's
Spirit in our lives.

—OR—

Response to the Word (Psalm 105, Philippians 1, Matthew 20)

Live your life in a manner worthy of the gospel.
We will be grateful for the food we eat.

We will thank God for clean water to drink.
Live your life in a manner worthy of the gospel.
We will be grateful for the opportunity to work.
We will thank God for our homes and our land.
Live your life in a manner worthy of the gospel.
We will be grateful for the Spirit's blessings.
We will thank God for choices that bring peace.

THANKSGIVING AND COMMUNION

Invitation to the Offering (Psalm 105)

In the wilderness of our lives, God's grace is like water gushing from a rock, transforming arid desert into a flowing river. In thanksgiving for God's mercy, let us give from our abundance as we collect today's offering.

Offering Prayer (Exodus 16, Philippians 1, Matthew 20)

Gracious God,
  you provide bread in the wilderness
    and life-giving waters in the desert;
  you offer work in the vineyard
    and community in the sanctuary.
In gratitude and thanks
  for your abundant gifts,
    accept our offering
      for the building of your realm:
        where all are fed,
        where all are clothed,
        and where all find purpose and passion,
          through Christ our Lord. Amen.

SENDING FORTH

Benediction (Matthew 20)

Go forth into the wilderness of life,
  trusting that we do not journey alone.
Drink of God's grace and eat your fill of God's love,
  for God nourishes us along the way!

(Mary J. Scifres)

CONTEMPORARY OPTIONS

Gathering Words (Exodus 16, Psalm 105, Matthew 20)
Manna from heaven in the morning...
God is in our midst.
Quail to eat in the evening...
God is in our midst.
Water gushing from a rock in the desert...
God is in our midst.
Work in the vineyard to feed our families...
God is in our midst.
Thanks be to God!

Praise Sentences (Psalm 105)
Sing to the Lord.
Sing praises to our God.
Praise the Lord for bread.
Praise God for life-giving waters.
Praise the Lord for home and land.
Praise God for work in the vineyard.
Praise the Lord!
Praise the Lord!
Praise the Lord!

SEPTEMBER 28, 2014

Sixteenth Sunday after Pentecost, Proper 21

B. J. Beu

COLOR

Green

SCRIPTURE READINGS

Exodus 17:1-7; Psalm 78:1-4, 12-16; Philippians 2:1-13; Matthew 21:23-32

THEME IDEAS

The saying "You had to be there to believe it" is an apt way of capturing the mood of today's Hebrew Scripture readings. The power of God is a fearful thing. Memories of God's mighty deeds of power are passed down in dark sayings of old, so says the psalmist. How do you convey the wonder and terror of water gushing from a rock on the mountain of God simply because Moses struck the rock with his staff? How do you convey the terror of a stiff-necked people who walked between the dangers of dying from hunger and thirst in the wilderness and of dying from snakebite at the hand of a God angered by their contemptuous lack of faith? God's power and authority are not hidden from those who have eyes to see and ears to hear. Yet we often shut our eyes and close our ears to the truth before us, as the chief priests and elders did in the presence of John the Baptist and Jesus. Philippians explains that Christ's power and authority came from his self-emptying and his willingness to become a servant for all. When we answer the call to serve, we are doing so by God's authority.

INVITATION AND GATHERING

Call to Worship (Psalm 78)

Give ear to God's teaching.
Incline your ears to parables and dark sayings of old.
We gather to hear the stories of our ancestors,
ancient stories of God's mighty deeds of power.
Do not hide them from your children.
Tell the coming generations of God's glorious deeds.
We gather to sing God's praises
and proclaim the wonders of our God.
Come to the fount of living water.
Drink deeply from the waters of life.
We gather to drink abundantly
from the wellspring of our salvation.
We gather as people reborn.

Opening Prayer (Exodus 17, Psalm 78)

Holy Mystery, grant us the courage to dive deep
into the teachings of our ancestors,
that we might fathom the depths
of dark sayings of old.
For we see in the stories of our ancestors
the truth we would deny in our own story.
We see your presence amidst their hopes and fears.
We see the courage it takes to truly lead.
We see the humility it takes to follow in faith.
We see life finding a way when all hope seems lost.
The whispered truths of the dark sayings of old
haunt our waking dreams,
telling us what our lives would become
if we but had the faith to believe.

We believe, Great Spirit.
Help our unbelief.

PROCLAMATION AND RESPONSE

Prayer of Confession (Exodus 17, Psalm 78, Philippians 2, Matthew 21)
God of second chances,
    forgive us when we grumble and groan,
      about our situation in life
        like the children of the Exodus;
    forgive us when we see your power in others
      as a challenge to our authority,
        like the chief priests and elders of old;
    forgive us for saying we will work in the vineyard,
      when we know we will not,
        like the son in Jesus' parable.
Make us one in your Spirit,
    and renew us in your compassion and grace,
      that our eyes may be opened to your presence
        and our minds may be filled
          with the very mind of Christ. Amen.

Words of Assurance (Psalm 78, Matthew 21)
Hear the good news:
    No matter who you are,
    or what you have done in your life,
    God's kingdom is open to all
    who hear the call to repentance
    and turn their lives back to God.
Be you tax collector or prostitute,
    bank robber or scam artist,
    the kingdom is available to all.
When we open our hearts and give our lives to Christ,
    God's forgiveness is truly ours.
Thanks be to God!

Passing the Peace of Christ (Philippians 2)
Make God's joy complete: Be of the same mind, have the
same love, and be in full accord with one another. In the

Spirit of God, which makes us one, turn and share signs of the peace of Christ.

Response to the Word (Philippians 2:5-7, 9; Matthew 21)
Hear again the words of Paul:
"Adopt the attitude that was in Christ Jesus: Though he was in the form of God, he did not consider being equal with God something to exploit. But he emptied himself by taking the form of a slave.... Therefore, God highly honored him and gave him a name above all names."
True authority and power comes from a life of servanthood. Likewise, our authority and power come from our willingness to serve others as we build the realm of God here on earth. So when God calls us into the vineyards of our lives, will we go or will we not? Our decision makes all the difference in the world.

THANKSGIVING AND COMMUNION

Invitation to the Offering (Philippians 2)
Paul exhorts: Let each of us look not to our own interests, but to the interests of others. In so doing, we share the mind of Christ. May we share generously of our gifts, and dedicate ourselves to lives of service and compassion as we gather today's offering.

Offering Prayer (Exodus 17, Philippians 2)
God of overflowing abundance,
    when your people suffered from thirst,
        you brought water from a rock
            to satisfy their need.
From the rock of your love, Holy One
    our blessings flow like ever-flowing streams.
Receive our thanks and praise
    for your many gifts.
Receive too our hearts, our hands,
    our dreams, our industry, and our love.
May our gifts draw us closer to you

and to one another,
   that we might all share
      the love and mind of the Lord. Amen.

Invitation to Communion (Exodus 17, Psalm 78)

This is the table of grace.
In Holy Communion:
   manna in the wilderness
      becomes the bread of life;
   water from a rock
      becomes the living stream of Christ's grace.
The promised land comes to us,
   that we might know Christ
      in the breaking of the bread
         and the sharing of the cup.
Come to the table of grace.
Drink of the promise of God.
Feed on the law of love,
   and your cup will be filled
      with a living water that never ends.

(Mary J. Scifres)

SENDING FORTH

Benediction (Philippians 2:1-2)

"If there is any encouragement in Christ,
   any comfort in love,
   any sharing in the Spirit, . . .
   complete [God's] joy
      by thinking the same way,
      having the same love,
      being united,
      and agreeing with each other."
Do this and you will live.

CONTEMPORARY OPTIONS

Gathering Words (Exodus 17)

Listen to parables and dark sayings of old.
   Tell us the stories of Jesus

and God's mighty deeds of power.
Consider well the fate of those who doubt our God.
Let us worship God, our Fount of living water.
We will worship the Lord,
the wellspring of our salvation.

Praise Sentences *(Psalm 78, Philippians 2)*

God's word inspires faith.
God's glory invites hope.
God's love brings joy.
God's Spirit offers life.
Give glory and praise to God.
Give glory and praise to God.
Give glory and praise to God.

OCTOBER 5, 2014

Seventeenth Sunday after Pentecost,
World Communion Sunday, Proper 22

Joanne Carlson Brown

COLOR
Green

SCRIPTURE READINGS
Exodus 20:1-4, 7-9, 12-20; Psalm 19; Philippians 3:4b-14;
Matthew 21:33-46

THEME IDEAS
The law, the teachings, the parables—these are easy to read,
but very hard to live authentically. In a society that values
individual freedom, law is a hard sell. But these are the very
teachings the world needs, not to curtail freedom but to enable us to be truly free in the life God offers. In a world of
violence, we need these words of guidance and radical,
transforming love. These are the words that can bind us together in spite of differences of language and custom. On
this World Communion Sunday, we rejoice and celebrate
the teachings that form the foundation of our life and faith.

INVITATION AND GATHERING

Call to Worship (Exodus 20, Psalm 19)
Come, people of God!
Come and hear the teachings of God.

We come with open hearts and minds,
ready to listen and obey.
God's teachings are perfect and sure, right and true.
We desire to live in the way.
Let us come with thanksgiving and joy.
Let us worship this God
who gives us wisdom, guidance, and truth.

Opening Prayer (Exodus 20, Psalm 19)

Giver of wisdom,
we come seeking guidance for our lives.
Open our minds to receive your teachings,
and open our hearts to treasure your precepts
as essential to our very existence.
Strengthen our faith through this time of worship
and through this time in community
with our sisters and brothers
who journey this path of life with us.
Let us taste the honey of your teachings
and your way. Amen.

PROCLAMATION AND PRAISE

Prayer of Confession (Exodus 20, Psalm 19, Matthew 21)

Merciful God, we live in a world that is beset with
violence, division, and greed.
Sometimes we get so swept up in the negativity
that we lose our way.
Sometimes we celebrate the things that separate us,
while ignoring those foundational things
that we have in common with one another.
We tell ourselves that our individual freedom
trumps any external law or teaching or demand.
Forgive our self-centeredness.
Forgive our desire to go it alone and have our own way.
Forgive our acquiescence to violence

and our resignation in the face of brute force
as the way to solve conflicts and problems.
Help us see your guiding words and teachings,
that we may walk the path of life
rather than the path of death.

Words of Assurance *(Exodus 20, Psalm 19)*
God loves us enough to give us teachings to live by.
If we embrace these teachings,
we will find abundant life.
If we embrace these teachings,
we will find sweetness of life.
If we embrace these teachings,
we will find God reaching out
in love and forgiveness, welcoming us home.

Passing the Peace of Christ *(Psalm 19)*
Greet one another with these words:
Rejoice! God is our rock and our redeemer.

Prayer of Preparation *(Psalm 19)*
Let the words of our mouths
and the meditations of our hearts
be acceptable to you, O God,
our rock and our redeemer.

Response to the Word *(Psalm 19)*
The law of God is perfect, reviving the soul.
The decrees of God are sure, making wise the simple.
Our hearts rejoice; our eyes are enlightened.
For this we give God thanks and praise.

THANKSGIVING AND COMMUNION

Invitation to the Offering *(Exodus 20, Psalm 19, Matthew 21)*
In a world of violence and division, a world that has lost its way, we can bring words of peace and healing. Our offering this day will enable this community to speak and live the teachings of life that offer guidance—teachings that offer the way.

Offering Prayer (Exodus 20, Psalm 19)
> For your teachings,
>> that are more to be desired than gold,
>>> and are sweeter than honey,
>>>> we give you humble thanks.
> For your many blessings,
>> we offer you our gold
>> and our selves in return.

SENDING FORTH

Benediction (Exodus 20, Psalm 19, Philippians 3)
> Follow the path of life laid out for you
>> in the sweet, golden teachings of our loving God.
> Go, sure of the value and life-giving gift
>> that is the knowledge of Jesus.
> Go, empowered by the Spirit
>> to live the way that leads to life and freedom. Amen.

CONTEMPORARY OPTIONS

Gathering Words (Exodus 20, Psalm 19)
> One God. No swearing. Honor your parents. No killing.
> No fooling around. No stealing. No lying.
> No looking with envy at what others have.
>> **Are you kidding?**
> No, these are words of life and truth.
> If we live these teachings
> the world will be a much better place.
>> **We'll need all the help we can get!**
>> **God better help us do that.**
> Then let's come before our God in prayer,
> with thanksgiving and confidence.
>> **Lead us, God, through this time of worship.**
>> **Help us live the way.**

Praise Sentences (Psalm 19)
> The heavens are telling the glory of God!
> The earth proclaims God's handiwork!
> God is our rock and our redeemer!

OCTOBER 12, 2014

Eighteenth Sunday after Pentecost,
Proper 23

Jamie D. Greening

COLOR
Green

SCRIPTURE READINGS
Exodus 32:1-14; Psalm 106:1-6, 19-23; Philippians 4:1-9;
Matthew 22:1-14

THEME IDEAS
The theme of worship surrounds both the record of the
golden calf incident in Exodus 32 and the poetic memory
of it in Psalm 106, although these are negative examples of
incorrect worship. Our beautiful Philippians passage uses
rich imagery calling us to focus upon God and the good
things of life. As such, Philippians 4:1-9 in this context is
an antidote for wrong worship in that it helps people turn
their thoughts, prayers, and giving to God, as they listen
to the right kinds of worship practices.

INVITATION AND GATHERING

Call to Worship (Philippians 4)
(Consider using a call-and-response format with a choir or a
group. This Call to Worship leads naturally into a musical piece
on the theme of rejoicing.)

Rejoice.
Rejoice?
Rejoice.
Rejoice.
Always.
Always?
Always.
Always.
For the Lord is near.
Near?
The Lord is near.
Always.
Rejoice!

Opening Prayer (Philippians 4)

Almighty God,
we open our service today seeking your help.
Help us think the right kinds of thoughts.
Help us think about things that are true and honorable,
things that are just, pure, and pleasing in your sight.
Help us focus on things that are commendable,
things that are excellent and worthy of praise.
There is so much in life that is unjust and ugly,
but we have gathered in your name this day
to commit ourselves to following your paths—
paths of justice and mercy,
paths that are worthy of your calling. Amen.

PROCLAMATION AND RESPONSE

Prayer of Confession (Psalm 106)

Praise the Lord,
for God is good!
(Pause.)
On this we rely,
for we have forsaken God's ways,
like our ancestors before us.
Our sins are the same.

We have worshiped idols of our own making—
   idols of money, possessions, and lust.
We have exchanged the glory of God
   for politics, power, and profit.
We have forgotten Christ our savior,
   and have turned our backs on God's love
      and our baptismal calling.
For these we offer our repentance,
   knowing that even in your righteous anger,
      you abound in steadfast love.
   (A time of silence may follow.)

Words of Assurance (Exodus 32)
For the Israelites of old, Moses stood in the breach,
   but for us there is a better mediator, Jesus Christ.
As we confess our sins,
   he stands today in the eternal breach of the cross
   to guarantee our forgiveness.

—OR—

Prayer of Confession (Exodus 32, Philippians 4)
Most Holy God,
   we have made gods out of gold and clay;
   we have allowed worries and doubts
      to cloud our vision and faith.
Do not think on these things, gracious God.
Find in us all that is honorable and true,
   commendable and excellent.
Shine in our lives,
   that we may reflect the just
      and righteous parts of ourselves.
Forgive us when we reflect false gods or sinful values.
Guide us back into your holy presence
   and transform us with your grace,
      that we may be the gentle and just people
         you would have us be and become.

(Mary J. Scifres)

Words of Assurance (Philippians 4)

The peace of God, which surpasses all understanding,
    is ours through Christ Jesus.
In Christ, we are forgiven indeed!

(Mary J. Scifres)

Passing the Peace of Christ (Philippians 4)

God's peace is a great blessing which transcends our understanding. In gratitude for this gift, let us bless one another with signs of God's peace.

Prayer of Preparation (Psalm 106)

Open our hearts, O Lord God,
    to feel your unending steadfast love.
Open our ears, O Lord God,
    to hear the mighty things you have done
        and are doing in our midst.
Open our eyes, O Lord God,
    to observe justice and righteousness.
Open our minds, O Lord God,
    to remember our deliverance from evil.

Response to the Word (Exodus 32, Psalm 106, Philippians 4)

When Aaron led the people to sin,
Moses stood in the breach
    between the people and God's wrath.
We have heard the word of the Lord.
May we not forget the lessons of our ancestors,
    nor neglect the work of the gospel
        as co-workers with God to bring the kingdom.

THANKSGIVING AND COMMUNION

Invitation to the Offering (Exodus 32, Psalm 106)

When the Israelites felt abandoned by God, they used their treasures of gold to make an idol to follow—an idol that would serve their needs. Let us today reject such foolish thinking and instead demonstrate proper stewardship

of God's blessings by returning to the Lord the prosperity
bestowed upon us.

Offering Prayer (Exodus 32, Psalm 106, Philippians 4)
Life-giving Lord,
 the Israelites took their gold
  and misused it for evil.
Today we offer you our gold and treasure
 in a desire to do good.
Redeem the folly of our selfishness
 and turn our gifts into joyous crowns.
May both our prosperity and our adversity
 be transformed into blessings for you
  and into a heritage for your people.
Use now these gifts
 to accomplish your purposes.

—OR—

Offering Prayer (Psalm 106, Philippians 4, Matthew 22)
God of steadfast love,
 we thank you for the abundant gifts in our lives:
  love and grace, clothing and belongings,
   friends and family.
We thank you for the steadfast signs
 of your loving presence in our world:
  wondrous works and awesome deeds.
We come before you with our offerings,
 rejoicing in this opportunity
  to help bring your realm here on earth.

(Mary J. Scifres)

SENDING FORTH

Benediction (Psalm 106, Philippians 4)
When you leave here today
 do not forget the wondrous works of the Lord.
Remember what you have learned and received
 as the God of peace goes with you.

CONTEMPORARY OPTIONS

Gathering Words (Philippians 4)

Women: Brothers, stand firm.

Men: Sisters, stand firm.

All: **Those loved by the Lord, stand firm.**

Men: Sisters, rejoice.

Women: Brothers, rejoice.

All: **We rejoice in the Lord.**

Women: Brothers, experience God's peace.

Men: Sisters, experience God's peace.

All: **Peace in our hearts,**
peace for our minds.

Praise Sentences (Psalm 106, Philippians 4)

Give thanks to the Lord, for God is good.
Grace is good.
Peace is good.
Joy is good.
God's steadfast love endures forever.
A love that does not end.
A love that does not end.
A love that does not end.

—OR—

Praise Sentences (Philippians 4)

Rejoice in God always! Again I say rejoice!
Rejoice in God always! Again I say rejoice!

(Mary J. Scifres)

OCTOBER 19, 2014

Nineteenth Sunday after Pentecost, Proper 24

Mary J. Scifres

COLOR

Green

SCRIPTURE READINGS

Exodus 33:12-23; Psalm 99; 1 Thessalonians 1:1-10; Matthew 22:15-22

THEME IDEAS

These disparate readings in the final days of the Ordinary Season can be challenging for both preacher and worship planner. Focusing on Matthew's story narrows today's theme. Jesus' encounters with the Pharisees challenge us to engage God's teachings more fully and to live God's teachings more completely. The Pharisees teach both the importance of returning first fruits to God and the need to avoid the idolatry of graven images and earthly values. In trying to trap Jesus, however, they forget the spirit of both laws. The point of God's teachings, whether they be the Ten Commandments, the Levitical code, or the parables of Jesus, is that God is our center and our source. When we remember and live this truth, returning first fruits to God and doing God's work in the world flows naturally. When we remember and live this truth, idolatry

fades away and we yearn only for further connection with
God. Centered on God, we can give God the same type of
faith and faithful Christian labor seen in the church at
Thessalonica.

INVITATION AND GATHERING

Call to Worship (Psalm 99, 1 Thessalonians 1)
O give thanks to God, who calls us here.
We will sing of God's glorious deeds.
O listen for God's wisdom, that speaks to us now.
We will listen for inspiration and truth.
O worship our God, who is holy and just.
We will worship God with honor and praise!

Opening Prayer (1 Thessalonians 1, Matthew 22)
Holy One, send your word, like rain in the desert,
    to satisfy our thirsty souls.
Nurture us and strengthen our spirits,
    that we may be centered on your ways
        and empowered by your Holy Spirit.
Inspire us to live your lessons,
    that our actions may be just
        and our words may be true reflections
            of your love and grace.
In your holy name, we pray. Amen.

PROCLAMATION AND RESPONSE

Prayer of Confession (Matthew 22)
God of justice and truth,
    you know the confusion of our minds
        and the hardness of our hearts.
When we seek to entrap,
    rather than to enlighten,
        forgive us.
When we obey the letter of the law
    and neglect the spirit of your love,
        forgive us.

When we lose focus,
 and forget to keep you at the center of our lives,
  bring us back to your truth.
Refocus our lives,
 that we may live as your followers,
  steadfast and true
   in all that we say and all that we do.
(A time of silent prayer may follow.)

Words of Assurance (1 Thessalonians 1)
The word of God has sounded forth:
 Jesus rescues us from all wrath
 and centers us in God's mercy and love.

Passing the Peace of Christ (1 Thessalonians 1)
With thanksgiving to God for the great works of faith and
the mighty labors of love in this community, let us share
our gratitude as we greet one another with signs of peace.

Prayer of Preparation (Matthew 22)
Teacher God,
 open our ears to hear your words;
 open our hearts to heed your wisdom.
Center us now,
 that we may find you,
  our one true Center,
   once again. Amen.

Response to the Word (Matthew 22)
(After each petition, a time of silence may follow.)
When we are trapped and confused,
 center us, O God.
When we idolize the rules and neglect your truth,
 center us, O God.
When we are held captive by our wealth and possessions,
 center us, O God.
When we return to you, looking for hope,
 center us, O God.
Center us, O God, with your mercy and love.
 Amen.

THANKSGIVING AND COMMUNION

Invitation to the Offering (Matthew 22:21)

Christ calls to us: "Give to God what belongs to God." All that we have and all that we are ... these are gifts from God, entrusted to us. Come, let us share these gifts with generosity and joy!

Offering Prayer (1 Thessalonians 1, Matthew 22)

Bless and increase the bounty of your love
    through the gifts we now give, O God.
Through these gifts and our faithful labors of love,
    may others come to know the steadfast hope
        and centering truth of your abundant grace.
In Christ's name, we pray.

SENDING FORTH

Benediction (1 Thessalonians 1)

With Christ as our center,
we are renewed in hope.
With Christ as our center,
we are called to serve.
With Christ as our center,
we are sent forth in love.

CONTEMPORARY OPTIONS

Gathering Words (1 Thessalonians 1, Matthew 22)

Which things are God's?
Which things are gods?
Which things are the world's?
Which things are the emperor's?
These questions challenge us,
calling us to center on the truth of God.
Love is of God. Hope is of God. Faith is of God.
These things abide,
centering and strengthening us
from age to age onward into eternity.

Praise Sentences (Psalm 99, Matthew 22)
God is our king of justice and love.
Praise God for justice and love!
God is the emperor of justice and love.
Praise God for justice and love!

OCTOBER 26, 2014

Twentieth Sunday after Pentecost,
Reformation Sunday, Proper 25
Hans Holznagel

COLOR
Green

SCRIPTURE READINGS
Deuteronomy 34:1-12; Psalm 90:1-6, 13-17;
1 Thessalonians 2:1-8; Matthew 22:34-46

THEME IDEAS
Today we observe the fine line between revering the past
and moving beyond it to the work at hand. The mourning
of the great prophet Moses comes to a definite end as his
successor, Joshua, leads on. Jesus declares love to be the
greatest commandment, then tries to dislodge the Pharisees from their focus on King David as the messianic an-
cestor. The psalmist, honoring God's presence to all
generations, ends with a prayer for the present: "Make the
work of our hands last."

INVITATION AND GATHERING

Call to Worship (Psalm 90)
O God, you have been our dwelling place
in every generation.
From everlasting to everlasting, you are God.

Before the mountains were brought forth,
or the earth had shape and form, you were there.
From everlasting to everlasting, you are God.
For a thousand years in your sight
are like a watch in the night.
From everlasting to everlasting, you are God.
Let us worship the everlasting God,
the God of yesterday, tomorrow, and today.

Opening Prayer (Deuteronomy 34, Psalm 90)

In remembrance of those
who have handed the faith down to us,
we give you thanks, O God.
Remembering that they did not stand still,
we ask that you move us forward
in faith and action.
O God of signs, wonders, and mighty deeds,
make your work clear and active through us. Amen.

PROCLAMATION AND RESPONSE

Prayer of Confession (Matthew 22, Deuteronomy 34, Psalm 90)

You make faith as simple
as loving you and our neighbors, O God.
Yet, we are sometimes tempted
to invent our faith as we go along.
When we become frail and our days are short,
we sometimes forget that you are with us now,
choosing to dwell instead
in the comfort of memories
of days long past.
Restore in us a faithful balance, we pray.
May love in the present be enough.
May faith be born of wisdom,
from saints who knew you,
even as we seek to know you,
face to face. Amen.

Words of Assurance (Psalm 90)
God is our dwelling place, our good news,
    our source of steadfast love.
In Christ we are restored and set aright. Amen.

Passing the Peace of Christ (Psalm 90)
Rejoicing now in God's steadfast love, let us share signs of
peace.
The peace of Christ be with you.
And also with you.

*Prayer of Preparation (Deuteronomy 34, Psalm 90,
Matthew 22)*
May the Spirit who guided faithful generations,
    be present in our midst this day
May God touch our hearts, souls, and minds
    with wisdom for life in these days. Amen.

Response to the Word (1 Thessalonians 2)
Entrusted with the message of the gospel,
    let us love deeply and act with courage
        in Christ's name. Amen.

THANKSGIVING AND COMMUNION

Invitation to the Offering (Deuteronomy 34)
Inspired by the witness of those who have gone before us,
grateful for the opportunities that lie before us now, let us
bring our tithes and offerings.

Offering Prayer (Psalm 90)
Let your favor, O God, be upon these gifts,
    that your work may prosper in this church,
        in this neighborhood,
            and in the wider world. Amen.

SENDING FORTH

Benediction (1 Thessalonians 2)
With God's love in your hearts,
    go forth sharing of yourselves,

living the good news,
and showing great affection
in this world that God loves. Amen.

CONTEMPORARY OPTIONS

Gathering Words (Deuteronomy 34)
It's a fine line.
We remember the heroes and the quiet ones,
   the ones who went before,
   the ones who made us what we are today.
But we, like them, can't stand still.
Remembering them, let's seek a faith for today—
   a faith of the here and now,
   a faith that moves us into the future.

Praise Sentences (Psalm 90, Matthew 22)
Hands.
   Hearts.
Minds.
   God, make them yours,
   and make them prosper!
Neighbors.
   Ourselves.
God.
   Let love prevail! Amen!

NOVEMBER 1, 2014

All Saints Day
Matthew J. Packer

COLOR
White

SCRIPTURE READINGS
Revelation 7:9-17; Psalm 34:1-10, 22; 1 John 3:1-3;
Matthew 5:1-12

THEME IDEAS
All Saints Day presents several possible themes: purity
(Revelation 7:14; Psalm 34:5; 1 John 3:3; Matthew 5:8);
worship (Revelation 7:9-12, Psalm 34:1-3); and present and
future hope. There is also an interesting juxtaposition between the lamb becoming the shepherd (Revelation 7:15-
17), and young lions (a symbol of strength) who suffer
want and hunger (Psalm 34:10). Finally, 1 John 3:2 holds
the promise of becoming like Christ, and Matthew 5:12
underscores a future reward for present suffering.

INVITATION AND GATHERING

Call to Worship (Psalm 34, Revelation 7)
*(Sing verse 1 of "For All the Saints" as an introduction to Call
to Worship.)*
I will bless the Lord at all times.
God's praise will continually be in my mouth!

O magnify the Lord with me,
and let us exalt God's name together!
We join with multitudes from every nation,
in praise to God and to the Lamb:
**Blessing and glory and wisdom
and honor and power and might,
be to our God forever and ever.**
(Sing verse 6 of "For All the Saints.")

Opening Prayer (Revelation 7)

Lord of the saints,
with the departed before your throne this day,
we lift up our hearts in thanksgiving and praise
for your gift of love in our lives.
We praise you especially
for the saving action of your Son, Jesus Christ.
By your Spirit,
draw us ever closer to you,
as we worship in communion with Christ,
with all who have gone before,
and with one another.
May we join with the saints and proclaim,
holy, holy, holy. Amen.

PROCLAMATION AND RESPONSE

Prayer of Confession (Matthew 5)

God of our mothers and fathers,
in your mercy and grace,
you offer us the life-transforming privilege
of becoming your children.
While we grow in likeness with Christ,
we humbly ask your forgiveness
for the times we have strayed
from the path you have set before us.
(silent prayer)
For the times we have neglected the poor,
Kyrie eleison, **Lord, have mercy.**

For the times we have failed to offer comfort,
Christe eleison, **Christ, have mercy.**
For the times we have taken advantage of the meek,
Kyrie eleison, **Lord, have mercy.**
For the times when we have persecuted the righteous,
Christe eleison, **Christ, have mercy.**
For the times we have failed to show mercy,
Kyrie eleison, **Lord, have mercy.**
For the times we have derided the pure of heart,
Christe eleison, **Christ, have mercy.**
For the times we have sought conflict instead of peace,
Kyrie eleison, **Lord, have mercy.**
For the times we have persecuted the righteous,
Christe eleison, **Christ, have mercy. Amen.**

Words of Assurance (Revelation 7, Psalm 34)

Scripture promises that the Lamb will be our shepherd,
  guiding us to springs of living water,
  and wiping away every tear from our eyes.
We serve a God who redeems God's servants,
  condemning none who seek refuge in God's fold.
To God and to the Lamb, let us sing,
  for in their name, we are forgiven.

Passing the Peace of Christ (1 John 3)

Beloved, we are God's children now. What we will be has
not yet been revealed. What we do know is this: When
Christ is revealed, we will be like him, for we will see him
as he is. Greet one another with the peace of Christ, recognizing the presence of Christ in each person you meet.

Introduction to the Word or Prayer of Preparation (1 John 3)

Faithful God, as your word is proclaimed,
  we pray for purity of heart, mind, and action.
Through the gift of your message,
  breathe your Spirit within our lives,
    in the name of the one who came
    to embody your word. Amen.

Response to the Word (Psalm 34)
Taste and see that the Lord is good.
Feasting on the truth and inspiration
of the word of God for the people of God.
Thanks and praise be to God.

THANKSGIVING AND COMMUNION

Invitation to the Offering (Psalm 34:9-10)
Hear the words of the psalmist: " You who are the LORD's
holy ones, honor [God because those who honor [God
don't lack a thing. Even strong young lions go without
and get hungry, but those who seek the LORD lack no good
thing." Let us give, trusting that God will generously provide for all of our needs, as we share with others the
wealth with which we have been entrusted.

Offering Prayer (Matthew 5, Revelation 7)
Giving God, you have blessed us beyond measure.
As we return a portion of your abundance,
we pray that you will multiply our gifts
to further your kingdom on earth
and transform our hearts and lives
for Jesus Christ.
We rejoice in anticipation of a great reward
in the kingdom to come:
communion with you
and fellowship with the saints and angels
for all eternity.
Until that day,
may your will be done,
on earth as it is in heaven. Amen.

SENDING FORTH

Benediction (Revelation 7)
Blessing and glory, wisdom and thanksgiving,
honor and power and might,
be to our God forever and ever!

Go in peace, lavished by the love of Christ,
    and surrounded by the great company of saints,
    to be a living beatitude to a hurting world. Amen.

CONTEMPORARY OPTIONS

Gathering Words (Psalm 34)

I sought the Lord and God answered me,
    delivering me from all my fears.
Let us lay aside all that hinders our worship,
    all that holds us back from experiencing
    the presence of Christ in our midst.
Let us enter joyfully into the house of the Lord,
    blessing God at all times
    with songs of continuous praise.

Praise Sentences (Psalm 34)

O magnify the Lord.
    God is worthy to be praised!
O magnify the Lord.
    God is worthy to be praised!

NOVEMBER 2, 2014

Twenty-first Sunday after Pentecost, Proper 26

B. J. Beu

COLOR

Green

SCRIPTURE READINGS

Joshua 3:7-17; Psalm 107:1-7, 33-37;
1 Thessalonians 2:9-13; Matthew 23:1-12

THEME IDEAS

Jesus sums up a major theme of today's scriptures: "But the one who is greatest among you will be your servant. All who lift themselves up will be brought low. But all who make themselves low will be lifted up" (Matthew 23:11-12). In Joshua, the priests bearing the ark of the covenant have to wade into the Jordan River before the waters part, allowing the people to walk across on dry ground. Jesus scolds the scribes and the Pharisees for forsaking servant ministry in favor of earthly recognition: the best seats in the synagogue, honor at banquets, and respect in the marketplaces. Paul reminds the church at Thessalonica that those who brought them the gospel worked day and night on their behalf so as not to be a burden on anyone. The psalmist describes the fate of the wicked and the righteous: The Lord turns the rivers of the wicked into parched ground, but transforms the deserts of the faithful into springs of water. Humility and gratitude for God's blessings lead to servant ministry and a recognition of our dependence on God, on one another, and on God's good earth.

INVITATION AND GATHERING

Call to Worship (Joshua 3, Psalm 107, Matthew 23)
Humble yourselves and listen for the word of God.
> **We gather to offer our service**
> **as we listen and pray.**

Humble yourselves and receive refreshment
from pools of living water.
> **We gather to bring comfort and solace**
> **to those who hunger and thirst.**

Humble yourselves and step into the river of faith.
> **We gather to help one another**
> **cross over the Jordan on dry ground.**

Come! Let us worship the Lord our God.
> **We come to worship God**
> **as we follow in the footsteps of Christ.**

Opening Prayer (Psalm 107, Matthew 23)
We sing your praises, O God,
> for your steadfast love endures forever.

When we are hungry and thirsty,
> you hear our cries
> > and deliver us from distress.

When our souls faint within us,
> you come to our aid
> > and revive us in pools of clear water.

Bless us with humility,
> that we may seek the welfare of others
> > before our own honor and glory.

May your love be our foundation,
> that our steps may never falter
> > as we seek the welfare of all. Amen.

PROCLAMATION AND RESPONSE

Prayer of Confession (Joshua 3, Psalm 107, Matthew 23)

Strong deliverer,
 it is not easy to humble ourselves before others
  and walk into the rivers of life,
   trusting that you will part the waters
    so others may cross on dry ground
     once we are wet.
We fear the ridicule of others,
 if the waters are not cut off
  and we find ourselves looking foolish
   rather than faithful.
We fear the loss of power and prestige,
 if we forsake the places of honor
  to claim the role of servant.
Heal us of our fears this day, O God,
 that we may live Christ's truth
  that the greatest among us are those who serve,
   and those who humble themselves
    will be exalted. Amen.

Words of Assurance (Joshua 3)

Sisters and brothers, draw near and know
 that miracles happen as surely today
 as they did in the time of our ancestors long ago.
Christ's grace saves us from our fears,
 and leads us into a freedom
 that the world cannot touch, much less take away.
Rest in the assurance of God's redeeming love.

Passing the Peace of Christ (1 Thessalonians 2)

As heirs with Christ, God calls us to lead lives worthy of our calling. Let us show ourselves worthy by offering one another signs of love and peace as we pass the peace of Christ.

Response to the Word (Joshua 3, Psalm 107, Matthew 23)

It wasn't until the soles of the feet of the priests
who bore the ark of God rested in the Jordan River
that the waters were cut off and the people were able
to walk across on dry ground.
**It isn't until the soles of our feet
enter the waters of servant ministry
that the word of God unfolds for us
and comes alive in our lives.**
Do not be hearers of the word only, but doers also.
**We offer our lives in humble service
to the Lord of life.**

THANKSGIVING AND COMMUNION

Invitation to the Offering (Psalm 107, Matthew 23)

The One who turns parched lands into springs of water,
the One who feeds the hungry from vineyards and fruit-
ful fields, calls us to work for the healing of our world. As
we collect this morning's offering, let us share generously,
that others may be touched by God's abundance.

Offering Prayer (Psalm 107)

Giver of all good things—
    for water that refreshes,
    for fields that yield their increase,
    and for the fruit of the vine
        that gladdens the heart;
            we offer you our thanks and praise.
May the fruit of our labor
    go forth into your world,
        and bless it with abundance.
May the gifts we bring this day
    be a source of refreshment and nourishment,
        like rivers in the desert,
            for those in need. Amen.

SENDING FORTH

Benediction (Joshua 3, Matthew 23)

Step confidently into the waters of grace.
God leads us into life.
Work humbly in the service of others.
Christ leads us into life.
Proclaim boldly the glory of our God.
The Spirit leads us into life.
Go with God's blessings.

CONTEMPORARY OPTIONS

Gathering Words (Psalm 107)

Deserts become pools of water.
Draw near to the God of love.
Parched land turns into springs of water.
Taste and see that God is good.
The hungry receive fields of plenty.
Surely the righteous will live.
The weary find rest.
Draw near to the God of love
and touch the peace
that passes all understanding!
Come! Let us worship the Lord of life.

Praise Sentences (Psalm 107)

Give thanks to the Lord, for God is good.
God's steadfast love endures forever.
Give thanks to Christ, our savior and teacher.
Christ's steadfast love endures forever!
Give thanks to the Lord, for God is good.
God's steadfast love endures forever.

NOVEMBER 9, 2014

Twenty-second Sunday after Pentecost, Proper 27

Mary J. Scifres

COLOR
Green

SCRIPTURE READINGS
Joshua 24:1-3a, 14-25; Psalm 78:1-7;
1 Thessalonians 4:13-18; Matthew 25:1-13

THEME IDEAS
What if the path to wisdom is simply constant preparation? If indeed the five bridesmaids with sufficient oil in
their lamps are "wise," and the unprepared bridesmaids
with insufficient oil are "foolish," then preparation is the
key to wisdom. Waiting for wisdom, and preparing for
spiritual growth, are not popular life paths today, nor
were they in Jesus' day. These last days of the Ordinary
Season lead us into a period of waiting and preparing for
Jesus' presence. The Advent season flies by far too quickly
in our fast-paced world to provide sufficient time or space
for the preparation our souls need to be filled and ready
to receive Christ's presence. If we begin to focus now and
to offer opportunities for waiting and preparing, we might
actually be ready to celebrate God's incarnation on Christmas Day. Wait for God. Prepare for the Christ child. Be

wise and fill your spiritual well deeply enough to withstand the dark days of December, the crazy demands of the holiday season, and the manic pace of life that pull us away from the true celebration of Christmas.

INVITATION AND GATHERING

Call to Worship (Matthew 25)
Wait for the Lord.
God is as near to us as our very breath.
Wait for God's wisdom.
Wisdom is planted in our very souls.
Prepare for the coming of Christ.
Christ lives in our very lives.
Wait, prepare, be ready to celebrate.
God is here, Christ has come.
Love is present here and now.

Opening Prayer (Matthew 25)
Christ, who is our Love and Life,
    wait with us now.
Prepare us to receive your presence.
Strengthen us to wait with perseverance and patience
    for the celebration of your place in our lives
        and your presence in our world.

PROCLAMATION AND RESPONSE

Prayer of Confession (Matthew 25)
Patient God, forgive our impatience.
Help us wait faithfully,
    as we prepare to hear and receive,
        not only your word,
            but your very presence in our lives
            and in our world.
Fill our lamps with your grace,
    that we might be ready to receive your forgiveness,
      and celebrate your unity with us.
In your holy name, we pray.

Words of Assurance (1 Thessalonians 4, Matthew 25)
Awake and alert, we are given new life in Christ,
strengthened by God's grace,
forgiven and reconciled by God's love,
to prepare anew for God's coming reign
in our world.

Passing the Peace of Christ (Matthew 25)
Wise or foolish, ready or not, all are welcome here. Turn to
your neighbors, sharing the oil of love and the balm of
grace, as we pass the peace of Christ this day.

Introduction to the Word (Matthew 25)
Keep your lamps lit and ready as you listen for the word
of God.

Response to the Word (Matthew 25)
Are you ready to move, prepared for the journey?
We are ready to walk with God!
Are you ready to serve, prepared to light the way?
We are ready to live in love!
Are you ready to celebrate, prepared to meet Jesus
in our world today?
**We are ready to celebrate God's presence
in every moment of our lives!**

THANKSGIVING AND COMMUNION

Invitation to the Offering (Matthew 25)
Whether wise or foolish, people need oil for their lamps.
People need food for their table and love for their lives.
Come, let us share the oil of our lives, that all may have
light for their way.

Offering Prayer (Matthew 25)
Loving God, receive these gifts of love,
as celebrations of your presence in our lives.
Shine through our gifts and our ministry,
that others may see light for their journey.

Live through our gifts and our ministry,
that all may experience and celebrate
your loving presence. Amen.

Invitation to Communion (Matthew 25)
Come to the banquet, Christ's banquet of love.
All are welcome here.
Come with your lights, ready and lit.
All are welcome here.
Come with your lamps, empty and dark.
All are welcome here.
Come to the banquet, for you will be filled.
All are welcome here.
Come to the banquet, Christ's banquet of love.
All are welcome here.

SENDING FORTH

Benediction (Matthew 25)
Keep awake! For darkness is all around!
May our hearts shine with God's love.
Keep awake! For the world is in constant need!
May we see and respond
where Christ calls us to serve.
As light for the world, go forth for God.
We go now to light the way!

CONTEMPORARY OPTIONS

Gathering Words (1 Thessalonians 4, Matthew 25)
Get ready, my friends. Christ is coming!
We are ready to receive our God!
Keep your lamps filled and ready!
We are ready to receive our God!
Change your light bulbs, replace those batteries.
We are ready to receive our God!
Get ready, my friends. Christmas is coming!
We are ready to receive our God!

Praise Sentences (Matthew 25)
Prepare the way, for God is here!
God is here today!
Prepare the way, with light and love!
God is here today!

NOVEMBER 16, 2014

Twenty-third Sunday after Pentecost,
Proper 28

B. J. Beu

COLOR

Green

SCRIPTURE READINGS

Judges 4:1-7; Psalm 123; 1 Thessalonians 5:1-11;
Matthew 25:14-30

THEME IDEAS

Themes of judgment and redemption unify today's readings. Judges recounts a familiar pattern: Israel sins, Israel
is delivered by God into the hand of a neighboring kingdom as punishment, Israel repents and returns to God's
precepts, God raises up a judge to rescue Israel. The
psalmist cries out for mercy to a God who hears our pleas.
The Epistle warns that the day of the Lord is coming like
a thief in the night, but that the righteous have nothing to
fear if they remain vigilant and faithful to God. Finally,
the Gospel recounts Jesus' parable of the talents and the
judgment God metes out based on how we use our gifts.
Here, redemption is tied to stewardship—it comes to
those who make the most of God's gifts, those who work
for the kingdom.

INVITATION AND GATHERING

Call to Worship (1 Thessalonians 5)
The day of the Lord comes
like a thief in the night.
We will remain vigilant
as children of the light.
A new day is dawning.
Forsake the ways of darkness.
We will live soberly
as children of the light.
Put on the breastplate of faith and love,
and the helmet of hope and salvation.
We will prepare ourselves
as children of the light.
Let us encourage one another
and build each other up.
We will work for the kingdom
as children of the light.

Opening Prayer (1 Thessalonians 5)
God of fall and winter, God of spring and summer,
you know the seasons of our lives.
Let the season of darkness and doubt pass away,
that we may be reborn in your light.
Lead us into a season of light and warmth:
a season of joy;
a season of sober judgment;
a season where all your children
are clothed in the breastplate of faith and hope,
and the helmet of hope and salvation.
Lead us into a season of kingdom building,
and we will put aside the ways of darkness
to live as children of light. Amen.

PROCLAMATION AND RESPONSE

Prayer of Confession (Matthew 25)
Faithful Steward,
you bless us with gifts

that are uniquely our own;
you bless us with talents
that are like pearls beyond price.
We should be amazed by the magnitude of your gifts,
but our talents seem so small in our eyes.
We should be grateful for the ways our talents fit us,
but our abilities seem awkward in our sight,
and the gifts of others
seem so much more desirable.
Clear our vision, Holy One,
and help us see the good to which
our talents and gifts may be put. Amen.

Words of Assurance (Matthew 25:23)

Do not fear, sisters and brothers in Christ,
for the One who blesses us with our gifts and talents
equips us for their use.
Look deep inside and know in your heart
that you have everything you need
to receive these words:
"Well done, good and trustworthy [servant];
you have been trustworthy in a few things,
I will put you in charge of many things;
enter into the joy of your master."

Passing the Peace of Christ (1 Thessalonians 5)

Called to live as children of light, let us encourage one another and build one another up as we share signs of peace
and words of love.

Introduction to the Word (Psalm 123, 1 Thessalonians 5)

Enthroned in the heavens,
God speaks to us on high.
Full of mercy and compassion,
God saves us from the contempt of the proud.
Hear words of promise and warning
from the One who is with us
in the bitter watches of the night.

We will listen to God's words,
and live as children of light.

Response to the Word (1 Thessalonians 5, Matthew 25)
Do you know what time it is?
It's time to wake up.
Do you know how late it is?
It's time to get going.
Do you know the night is over?
It's time to live as children of light.
Do you know what it's time to do?
**It's time to trust God's love
and answer Christ's call!**

THANKSGIVING AND COMMUNION

Invitation to the Offering (1 Thessalonians 5, Matthew 25)
For it is as if our God, going on a journey, summoned Christ's followers and entrusted all of God's earth to them. We are the trustees of all that God has given us. Let us share these gifts in faith and trust, in courage and hope, as signs of light and love.

(Mary J. Scifres)

Offering Prayer (1 Thessalonians 5, Matthew 25)
Giver of gifts,
    you know the true value
        of the talents you bestow upon us.
Open our eyes
    to see the possibilities
        they hold for our world.
Transform the gifts we offer this day
    into signs of our commitment
        to bring light and love
            to every task we do.
Transform our understanding of our potential,
    that we may shine forth:
        as children of light,
        as people of faith,

and as bearers of hope,
    through Christ our Lord,
       who loves and strengthens us. Amen.

SENDING FORTH

Benediction (1 Thessalonians 5)
Clothed in faith and showered in love,
    we go forth shining with God's light.
Washed in joy and bathed in the hope of our salvation,
    we go forth radiant with Christ's love.
Blessed with gifts far more precious than jewels,
    we go forth blazing with the fire of God's Spirit.

CONTEMPORARY OPTIONS

Gathering Words (Matthew 25)
God has richly blessed you...
use your gifts to build God's kingdom.
    But we're afraid.
God has richly blessed you...
find your courage and don't look back.
    But our gifts seem so small.
God has richly blessed you...
you possess everything you need.
    But what if we fail?
God has richly blessed you...
trust the gifts you have been given.
    We will use our gifts.
    Thanks be to God!

Praise Sentences (Judges 4, 1 Thessalonians 5, Matthew 25)
Praise God who shines light in our darkness.
    Praise God who brings victory out of defeat.
Praise God who turns mourning into dancing.
    Praise God who bestows gifts beyond price.
Praise God.
    Praise God.
Praise God.

NOVEMBER 23, 2014

Reign of Christ/Christ the King Sunday, Proper 29
Rebecca Gaudino

COLOR
White

SCRIPTURE READINGS
Ezekiel 34:11-16, 20-24; Psalm 100; Ephesians 1:15-23; Matthew 25:31-46

THEME IDEAS
God is wholly involved in our world. Ezekiel describes God as being among the scattered, injured sheep of Israel, and Ephesians describes Christ as the one who "fills everything in every way" (v. 23). At the same time, today's texts describe God as enthroned above our world—beyond the day-to-day goings-on in our world, apart from the scattering and injuring, the binding up and gathering. These texts invite and challenge us to step back and look with clear eyes at who we are as the Church in this world, then to live like Jesus, enacting the hope, riches, and immeasurably great power of God "among us believers" (Ephesians 1:19) on behalf of God's world.

INVITATION AND GATHERING

Call to Worship (Psalm 100)
(Use music throughout this Call to Worship: A cantor could chant the words of the psalm quoted here, leading to a

well-known chorus or hymn stanza. Musicians could play softly behind a reader's spoken words and then swell for the congregation's singing. Musicians could respond to each of the first two praise sentences in the two triplets, perhaps with the opening line of the upcoming hymn, played with some flourish! Then the congregation would join in after each of the third praise sentences.)

Make a joyful noise to the Lord, all the earth!
(musical response)
Worship the Lord with gladness!
(musical response)
Come into God's presence with singing!
(Sing a chorus or verse of a well-known hymn or a doxology.)
Enter God's gates with thanksgiving
and these courts with praise.
(musical response)
Give thanks to God, bless God's holy name!
(musical response)
Come into God's presence with singing!
(Sing the same chorus or verse.)

Opening Prayer (Psalm 100, Ephesians 1, Matthew 25)

Jesus Christ, our sovereign,
who is seated above all powers
in the heavenly places,
we worship you with gladness,
for you are over all things,
the head of the Church.
Jesus Christ, Son of Man,
who stands with us when we are hungry and sick,
we give you thanks and bless your name.
We come to you,
you who are enthroned above all,
even as you stand among us,
and we thank you for your faithfulness
to all generations. Amen.

PROCLAMATION AND RESPONSE

Prayer of Confession (Ezekiel 34, Matthew 25)

Sovereign Christ, Shepherd King,
    you seek the lost and the hurting,
        the strayed and the weary.
We can see you kneeling beside the injured,
    and we ask for your strong and tender hands
        to bind up our injuries, and carry us to safety.
We also ask your forgiveness
    when we have injured others
        and scattered the weak,
    when we have forgotten that *we* are your strong
        and tender hands in this world.
Forgive us, and renew us,
    that we may accomplish your saving work
        in the world. Amen.

Words of Assurance (Psalm 100, Ephesians 1)

God's steadfast love endures forever!
Because of this love, we are forgiven.
Because of this love, we receive the rich
    and glorious inheritance of God's life and power.
Through Jesus our sovereign,
    who sits at the right hand of God,
    we receive life beyond measure.
Give thanks to God!

Passing the Peace of Christ (Matthew 25)

When we look into the face of our brothers and sisters, we
look into the face of Jesus himself. So look with new eyes,
and see Jesus as you welcome your brothers and sisters in
Christ.
    The peace of Christ be with you!

Prayer of Preparation (Ephesians 1)

God of glory, God of our sovereign Jesus Christ,
    give us a spirit of wisdom and revelation
        as we come to know you more deeply.

With the eyes of our hearts enlightened,
    may we know the hope
        to which you have called us. Amen.

Response to the Word (Psalm 100, Ephesians 1)
Grant us your wisdom, O God.
Reveal to us your steadfast love
    at work in our world.
Keep our hope alive,
    that we may never doubt
        your astonishing power! Amen.

THANKSGIVING AND COMMUNION

Invitation to the Offering (Ephesians 1, Matthew 25)
We have received lavish riches of love and hope from God
through Jesus Christ. Let us give our offerings today out
of that same love and hope, so that others—the hungry,
the sick, the imprisoned—may experience this same love
and hope. Through our giving, may all know that we, the
Church, are Jesus standing with them.

Offering Prayer (Ezekiel 34, Ephesians 1, Matthew 25)
Sovereign Christ, Shepherd King,
    work your great power
        in immense and tender ways
            in our world.
Use us, and use our gifts
    on behalf of the least of these:
        to seek the lost,
        to bring back the strayed,
        to bind up the injured,
            and to strengthen the weak.
May no one feel like a stranger in our midst,
    but may all know that they are
        our brothers and our sisters.
Through our gifts and our very lives,
    may we be your body, Jesus,
        the presence of your powerful love—
            a love that heals our world. Amen.

SENDING FORTH

Benediction (Ephesians 1)
We, who are standing here,
are the body of Jesus in this world!
So go in the hope and love
and the immeasurably great power
of Jesus Christ!

CONTEMPORARY OPTIONS

Gathering Words (Psalm 100, Ezekiel 34)
God, you rescue us when we become lost.
You gather us from wayward paths.
You bind up our injuries,
and strengthen us when we're weak.
We know that you are our God,
for we are your people.
You love us through thick and thin!
**And so, we come into your presence this day
with praise and singing!**

Praise Sentences (Psalm 100)
Make a joyful noise to God, all the earth!
**Wind, blow through the trees
and let us hear your singing!**
Sea, dash those waves upon the shores!
Birds, show us how to really twitter!
Lions and wolves, roar and howl!
Cows and sheep, moo and baa!
Babies and children, laugh with joy!
Shout a great shout, people of God.
Make a joyful noise to God, all the earth!

NOVEMBER 27, 2014

Thanksgiving Day

Deborah Sokolove

COLOR
White

SCRIPTURE READINGS
Deuteronomy 8:7-18; Psalm 65; 2 Corinthians 9:6-15;
Luke 17:11-19

THEME IDEAS
Thanksgiving is a time to reflect upon our many blessings.
Deuteronomy reminds us that God is the source of all our
blessings and warns us not to take credit for our wealth
and success. The psalmist affirms that God crowns the
year with bounty; Paul urges us to be cheerful givers; and
Jesus challenges us to praise God for all our blessings.

(B. J. Beu)

INVITATION AND GATHERING

Call to Worship (Psalm 65)
Come, let us give our praises to God.
We come to the One who answers prayer.
Happy are those whom God has chosen.
**We shall be satisfied with the goodness
of God's presence.**

—OR—

Call to Worship (Deuteronomy 8, Psalm 65)
Come to the Lord with praise and thanksgiving.
Worship God with gladness.
Come to the Lord with gratitude and joy.
Shower God with praise.
Come to the Lord with grateful hearts.
Love God with humility.
Come! Worship the Lord.

(B. J. Beu)

Opening Prayer (Deuteronomy 8)
Extravagant, generous giver of all good things,
    just as you brought the Israelites
        into a land flowing with milk and honey—
            a land where they could be free
                from bondage and oppression,
you have brought us into this good land—
    a land with flowing streams,
        with springs and underground waters
            welling up in valleys and hills,
    a land of wheat and corn, of fertile plains,
        and majestic mountains.
We give you thanks:
    for the bounty that fills our tables,
    for the water that satisfies our thirst,
    for the beauty of this land
        where we are free to worship you
            in the name of Jesus, who is the Christ. Amen.

PROCLAMATION AND RESPONSE

Prayer of Confession (Deuteronomy 8)
Praise is due to you, O God.
**But in our pride, we forget you,
    believing that our successes
    are due to our own power.**
Praise is due to you, O God.
But we exalt ourselves, instead,

forgetting that you have freed us
to find our life in you.
Praise is due to you, O God.
**Forgive us when we rely on our own strength,
instead of yours.**

Words of Assurance (2 Corinthians 9)
The Holy One provides us with every blessing
in abundance, forgiving us even before
we remember to give thanks.
In the name of Christ, you are forgiven.
**In the name of Christ, you are forgiven.
Glory to God. Amen.**

*Passing the Peace of Christ (Deuteronomy 8,
Psalm 65, 2 Corinthians 9)*
In gratitude for the astonishing gifts of God, let us ex-
change signs of peace with one another.
The peace of Christ be with you.
The peace of Christ be with you always.

Response to the Word (2 Corinthians 9, Luke 17)
Like the Samaritan who was healed by Jesus, let us always
praise God for the surpassing grace that has been given to us.

THANKSGIVING AND COMMUNION

Invitation to the Offering (2 Corinthians 9)
In gratitude for God's grace, let us bring our gifts and offerings before the Lord this day.

Offering Prayer (2 Corinthians 9, Luke 17)
Generous Healer of all who ask for mercy,
you alone supply seed to those who sow
and turn it into bread for food.
Accept our gifts for the needs of your saints,
and for the healing of your world. Amen.

Great Thanksgiving
Christ be with you.
And also with you.

Lift up your hearts.
  We lift them up to God.
Let us give our thanks to the Holy One.
  It is right to give our thanks and praise.

It is a right, good, and joyful thing,
    always and everywhere to give our thanks to you,
    who have brought us into a land of plenty
    and filled us with every good thing.
We give you thanks and praise
    for bringing our ancestors out of bondage,
    leading them through the dangerous wilderness,
    giving them water from flinty rock,
    and feeding them on manna from your hand.
And so, with your creatures on earth,
    and all the heavenly chorus,
    we praise your name and join their unending hymn:
    Holy, holy, holy Lord, God of power and might,
      heaven and earth are full of your glory.
    Hosanna in the highest. Blessed is the one
      who comes in the name of the Lord.
    Hosanna in the highest.

Holy are you, and holy is your child, Jesus Christ.
    who heals the broken,
    and teaches us to be generous to all.
On the night in which he gave himself up,
    Jesus took bread, gave thanks to you,
    broke the bread, and gave it to the disciples, saying:
"Take, eat; this is my body which is given for you.
Do this in remembrance of me."
When the supper was over, Jesus took the cup,
    offered thanks, and gave it to the disciples, saying:
"Drink from this, all of you;
    this is my life in the new covenant,
    poured out for you and for many,
    for the forgiveness of sins.

Do this, as often as you drink it,
in remembrance of me."
And so, in remembrance of your mighty acts
in Jesus Christ . . . we proclaim the mystery of faith:
Christ has died.
Christ is risen.
Christ will come again.

Pour out your Holy Spirit on us gathered here,
and on these gifts of bread and wine.
Make them be for us the body and blood of Christ,
that we may be the body of Christ
to a broken, hurting world.
Spirit of abundant life, Healer of the sick, Creator of all,
we praise your holy, eternal name. **Amen.**

SENDING FORTH

Benediction (2 Corinthians 9)
Give thanks to God in all that you do,
for all that you have,
for every moment of your lives.
God provides you with every blessing,
so that you may share it abundantly
with all the world. **Amen.**

CONTEMPORARY OPTIONS

Gathering Words (Psalm 65)
Happy are those whom God has chosen.
We come to the One who answers prayer.

—OR—

Gathering Words (Deuteronomy 8)
Praise God for flowing streams!
Our God is an awesome God!
Praise God for wheat and barley, iron and copper!
Our God is an awesome God!

Praise God for the commandments that lead to life!
Our God is an awesome God!
Praise God who provides for us!
Our God is an awesome God!

(B. J. Beu)

Praise Sentences (Psalm 65, 2 Corinthians 9)
Come, let us give our praises to God.
Thanks be to God for so many indescribable gifts!

NOVEMBER 30, 2014

First Sunday of Advent
(Begin Lectionary Year B)

J. Wayne Pratt

COLOR

Purple

SCRIPTURE READINGS

Isaiah 64:1-9; Psalm 80:1-7, 17-19; 1 Corinthians 1:3-9; Mark 13:24-37

THEME IDEAS

The season of Advent proclaims the coming of Christ, whose birth we prepare to celebrate once again, and whose return in final victory we anticipate. In today's lessons, the prophet Isaiah calls on God to "tear open the heavens," that the nations might tremble and confess their need for divine intervention. The psalmist urges the people to cry out for restoration from exile, and to seek the light of God's salvation. Paul likewise points to the end times and the coming Day of the Lord, urging Jesus' followers to faithfully share their spiritual gifts. In the Gospel text, Jesus cautions his followers to be alert and to watch for signs of the end times and Christ's return in glory.

INVITATION AND GATHERING

Call to Worship (Isaiah 64)

Isaiah pleads for God to open the heavens
and come down.

The mountains quake at God's presence.
God embraces those who do right and seek justice,
those who walk in godly ways.
Like clay in the hands of the potter,
we are the work of God's creative hand.
We are all God's people.
God is slow to anger,
abounding in steadfast love.

—OR—

Call to Worship (Mark 13)
When is the Master coming?
No one knows the day or the hour.
When must we be ready to receive the Lord of hosts?
Even now, listen for the knock on the door.
Keep alert and be ready.
We await the one who brings us life.

(*B. J. Beu*)

Opening Prayer (Mark 13, 1 Corinthians 1)
God, your promise of hope comes to us,
wrapped in anticipation and expectation.
Though the sun may be darkened,
though the moon may cease to give forth its light,
though the stars may fall from heaven,
we will continue to thank you
that a new day is dawning—
a day when we will see the Son of Man
coming with power and glory.
As we await that day with great hope,
may we use our spiritual gifts to your glory.
Reveal to us our Lord Jesus Christ,
that we may be strengthened
and blameless in your sight.
You are faithful, Lord;
may it be so for us who have gathered
in your name. Amen.

PROCLAMATION AND RESPONSE

Prayer of Confession (Isaiah 64, Psalm 80, Mark 13)

O God of new seasons and vibrant possibilities,
we often hide from times of new growth
and transformation.
At a time when we should burst forth with new life,
we fade like autumn leaves
touched by a cold, north wind;
we hibernate like bears in winter,
waiting for the spring thaw.
Do not be angry, Lord,
and remember our sins no more,
but come and save us.
Tear open the heavens and come down.
Make your presence known,
and let your face shine upon us
that we may be saved.

Words of Assurance (Mark 13)

God calls us to be watchful,
awakened to new possibilities
and vibrant growth.
Know that God forgives our sins
and restores us to kingdom living.
We are recreated in God's holy image.
With growth in the Spirit,
we know that God is so very near.

Passing of the Peace

God's shining face and comforting embrace come into the
world, that we may know the love of Christ. See this love
in one another as we share signs of Christ's peace.

Words of Preparation or Words of Affirmation (Mark 13)

Christ has died. Christ has risen.
Christ will come again.
Keep awake, for we do not know

when the master will come.
Christ has said to all: "Keep awake."

Response to the Word (Mark 13)

We hear God's word to be alert, to keep awake, for we know not when the time will come. The Son of Man will come in the clouds with great power and glory, sending out the heavenly angels to gather God's elect from the ends of the earth and from the farthest reaches of heaven. Through God's word, the church puts forth its roots and leaves to become the gateway for God to stand near. Heaven and earth may pass away, but God's words will endure forever. May it be so for each of us.

THANKSGIVING AND COMMUNION

Invitation to the Offering (1 Corinthians 1)

Paul offers thanks to God for the grace and spiritual gifts that have been given, that we may not be found lacking. In joyful appreciation of God's faithful gifts, let us now offer back to God the gift of our hearts, our tithes, and our offerings. As we have freely received, so now let us freely give.

Offering Prayer (1 Corinthians 1)

God of all creation,
    you have blessed each and every one of us,
        not only with spiritual gifts,
            but with the resources we need
                to follow the precious gift of your Son.
We stand on the advent of anticipation,
    for you have given us the gift of life,
        sustained us with heavenly nourishment,
        and embraced us with your love.
May the offering we collect this day
    be blessed and used in mission and ministry,
        to glorify your holy name.
In Jesus' name we pray. Amen.

—OR—

Offering Prayer (Mark 13)

Although we do not know
    the day or time of your coming, dear God,
we know that now is the time
    to be your children of light.
Receive the gifts we bring.
Transform them into light for the world,
    into signs of peace and hope for all to see. Amen.

(Mary J. Scifres)

Invitation to Communion

O God of new beginnings and transformed lives,
    you call us to be alert and watchful
        for your coming kingdom.
As we gather at this your table, Lord,
    we pray that you would meet us in this sacred meal.
Restore us to the fullness of your love,
    and guide us to be the image of Christ
        in the world today.
Unite us and join us together
    as the body of Christ.
Shine in and through us,
    that we may be light to those around us.
Transform us through this meal
    to be grace-filled and grace-giving children
        of your mercy.
Fill us with hope, love, and justice,
    in Jesus' name we pray.
Come. Come and share in the advent feast of our Lord.

SENDING FORTH

Benediction

Our journey to Bethlehem has begun,
and soon God's glory will be fully revealed.
    **We watch, we wait, and we anticipate
    Christ's coming into our lives.**

May the light of God's glory
shine brightly in your lives,
and may you seek to be a beacon of hope
for those who walk in darkness.
> **We go from this house of God
> into the world of God's creation,
> beckoning others to a journey of new beginnings.**

CONTEMPORARY OPTIONS

Gathering Words (Mark 13)

One in hope, one in faith, and one in baptism,
> **we gather from the four winds
> to center our lives in Christ.**

From the ends of the earth to the ends of heaven,
> **we gather to praise God
> who is coming to us
> in clouds of power and glory.**

The Master of the house invites us
to embark on the amazing journey of Advent.
> **Along this journey we pause to worship our God.**

Praise Sentences (Psalm 80)

God restores our life.
God hears our prayers.
God saves us from our sins.
God's face shines upon us.
God restores our life.

(B. J. Beu)

DECEMBER 7, 2014

Second Sunday of Advent

Amy B. Hunter

COLOR

Purple

SCRIPTURE READINGS

Isaiah 40:1-11; Psalm 85:1-2, 8-13; 2 Peter 3:8-15a;
Mark 1:1-8

THEME IDEAS

As wonderful as it is to ponder God coming to us as a
helpless infant, Advent is much more than remembering
the birth of Jesus. Today's readings call us to live in hope
of the fulfillment of God's vision for humanity and creation. The prophet Isaiah and the psalmist remember
God's decisive action of bringing the Hebrew people out
of exile. Yet these same people struggle with disappoint-
ment as they find the work of restoration grueling and
seemingly unrewarding. The epistle calls for hope as the
early Christian community struggled; Jesus had not re-
turned to make everything right. Advent recalls God's
blessing in our past, even as we seek to know God's presence here and now in our ordinary lives. Advent demands
that we see our lives, our world, and all reality through
God's eyes, that we may long for what God desires: for all
things to be made new and whole. Into this whirl of
human memory, need, and hope steps the wonderful

figure of John the Baptist, who reminds us that Jesus is knocking at the door, ready to enter our world.

INVITATION AND GATHERING

Call to Worship (Isaiah 40, Psalm 85, Mark 1)

In the wilderness of our daily lives, a voice cries out:
Prepare the way of the Lord.
Let us hear what God is saying.
God has shown us favor by restoring our fortunes.
Let us rejoice in what God is doing.
God rules this world with tenderness and might.
Let us share what God is offering.
The glory of the Lord will be revealed.
Let all people see it and turn their hearts to God.
Let us proclaim what God is bringing.
In the wilderness of our daily lives, a voice cries out:
Prepare the way of the Lord!

Opening Prayer (Isaiah 40, Psalm 85, 2 Peter 3, Mark 1)

Lord God, in this season of Advent
  remind us that we have always been your people—
  a people you created, called, and redeemed.
  Having love for all people,
    we thank you for your favor.
Remembering our sacred story,
  may we look for your presence in our world today.
  Surely salvation is at hand
    for those who turn to you in love.
  Surely your glory dwells with us here,
    through Jesus Christ, our Lord.
Seeing your presence among us now,
  may we remember that we are an Advent people
  who wait for your kingdom to be revealed.
  We long for the day
    when righteousness will be established,
    and your Advent promise will be fulfilled.

Prepare us, O Lord,
   that we may become your instruments
   of grace and mercy in the world! **Amen.**

PROCLAMATION AND RESPONSE

Prayer of Confession (Isaiah 40, Psalm 85, 2 Peter 3)
   God of endless mercy, hear our prayer:
   You have comforted us,
      you have cared for us tenderly,
      and you have restored our losses.
   Yet we wither like grass
      when winter winds blow upon it.
   We fade like cut flowers in a vase,
      beautiful but for a few short days.
   You speak peace to us
      and call us to be faithful,
         yet we turn away from you,
            choosing folly, strife,
               and passing pleasures.
   You are patient with us,
      yet we accuse you of apathy and neglect.
   Forgive us, we pray.
   Make us mindful of our salvation through Jesus Christ,
      who was, and is, and is to be—
         the one who is eternally transforming us
            through the power of your Holy Spirit. Amen.

Words of Assurance (Isaiah 40, Psalm 85, 2 Peter 3)
   God desires that all may live in fullness of life.
   God longs for all people to come to repentance,
      that they may see the glory of God
      revealed in our savior Jesus Christ.
   And so, God speaks tenderly with us
      and hurries to comfort us.
   Be assured of God's favor,
      and know that our sin has been forgiven. Amen.

Passing the Peace of Christ (2 Peter 3)

Beloved people of God, trusting in the grace of Jesus Christ, we wait for a new creation and for God's realm, where righteousness is at home. While we wait, let us treasure God's patience with us, and let us always be at peace with God and with one another. Greet one another with signs of our faith as we share the peace of Christ.

Introduction to the Word or Prayer of Preparation (Isaiah 40)

All people are like grass,
and like the flowers of the field.
The grass withers, the flowers fade,
but the word of our God endures forever.

Response to the Word (Isaiah 40)

Prepare the way of the Lord.
Make straight a highway for our God.
Then the glory of the Lord shall be revealed,
and all people shall see it together.
The word of our God shall stand forever.

THANKSGIVING AND COMMUNION

Invitation to the Offering (Isaiah 40, Psalm 85)

Let us offer our gratitude for God's countless blessings: past, present, and future in God's eternal kingdom.

Offering Prayer (Isaiah 40, 2 Peter 3, Mark 1)

Lord God, you have shown us your glory:
in your holy word,
in the blessings of our daily lives,
and in the promise of your eternal kingdom.
You share your glory with us,
giving us the power to live
in holiness and godliness.
Your loving patience gives us hope
as we await the coming of your Son, Jesus Christ.
In gratitude and thanks,

we offer you our hearts, our lives,
    and all that we have.
Use these gifts, we pray,
    to prepare your way of salvation
    and to establish your realm of peace.
This we ask in the name of Jesus Christ. Amen.

SENDING FORTH

Benediction (Isaiah 40, Psalm 85, 2 Peter 3, Mark 1)
    Get up to a high mountain, people of God,
    you are the heralds of God's good tidings.
        We will proclaim the way of the Lord, saying:
        Here is your God!
    Tell everyone the story of God's blessings
    in Jesus Christ.
        We will proclaim the way of the Lord, saying:
        Here is your God!
    God comes to us with might, bringing glory
    and redemption.
        We will proclaim the way of the Lord, saying:
        Here is your God!
    God entreats us with tenderness and patience,
    establishing peace.
        We will proclaim the way of the Lord, saying:
        Here is your God!
    Go forth rejoicing, as heralds of God's good tidings.
        We will proclaim the way of the Lord, saying:
        Here is your God!

CONTEMPORARY OPTIONS

Gathering Words (Isaiah 40, Psalm 85, 2 Peter 3)
    You who proclaim God's glory,
    remember the blessings of days gone by.
        Jesus is coming to show us God's glory!
    Sisters who sing God's glory,
    listen, for God is speaking to us today.

Jesus is coming to show us God's glory!
Brothers who shout God's glory,
rejoice in God's patience as you await God's holy day.
Jesus is coming to show us God's glory!
We are the people who proclaim God's glory.

Praise Sentences (Isaiah 40, Psalm 85)

Praise to our God who comes to us!
Give thanks and see God's glory.
God's faithfulness springs up from the ground.
God's righteousness showers us from above.
Praise to our God who comes to us!
Give thanks and see God's glory.

—OR—

Praise Sentences (Isaiah 40, Psalm 85)

Lift up your voice with strength.
Sing of God's glory and grace!
Lift up your voice with strength.
Sing of God's glory and grace!

(Mary J. Scifres)

DECEMBER 14, 2014

Third Sunday of Advent

B. J. Beu

COLOR

Purple

SCRIPTURE READINGS

Isaiah 61:1-4, 8-11; Psalm 126; 1 Thessalonians 5:16-24; John 1:6-8, 19-28

THEME IDEAS

The One who restores Israel is the One who brings good news: release to the captives, help to the oppressed, and joy to the brokenhearted. The One who restored Israel's fortunes in the time of Isaiah is the One who sent John to make straight the way of the messiah. Now is the time to rejoice, to pray without ceasing, and to prepare for our salvation.

INVITATION AND GATHERING

Call to Worship (Psalm 126, Isaiah 61)
When the Lord restored our fortunes,
we were like those who dream.
**Our mouths were filled with laughter,
our tongues with shouts of joy.**
Restore our fortunes once more, O God,
that our tears may turn into shouts of joy,

our weeping may give rise to singing.
Come worship the Lord
who clothes us with the garments of salvation.
Worship the Lord!

Opening Prayer (Psalm 126, Isaiah 61)
God of Dreams, from times of old,
    you have done great things for your people.
Awaken us to the dawn of your glory.
Fill our mouths with laughter,
    our tongues with shouts of joy.
Anoint us with your oil of gladness
    and give us a garland instead of ashes.
May we be known among all people
    as oaks of righteousness,
        the plantings of the Lord. Amen.

PROCLAMATION AND RESPONSE

Prayer of Confession (John 1, Isaiah 61)
Merciful God, after two thousand years,
    we still don't quite know
        what we're looking for.
We have heard John's fervent cry in the wilderness:
    "Make straight the way of the Lord,"
        but we're unsure what you want us to do.
Our lives have continued on
    much as they were before.
We have not listened to your heralds
    and have not lived as if we truly believe.
Forgive us, Holy One.
Help us hear anew
    the cry of those who lead us in the ways of life.
Tune our ears to your heralds,
    that we too might testify to your light. Amen.

Words of Assurance (1 Thessalonians 5)
May the God of peace sanctify you,
    that your spirit and soul

may be kept sound and blameless.
The One who calls us is faithful
and fashions us for the life
that truly is life.

Passing the Peace of Christ (Isaiah 61)
Clothed by God in the garments of salvation and the robes
of righteousness, let us celebrate the fabric of God's love
in our lives by sharing signs of the peace of Christ.

Response to the Word (1 Thessalonians 5, John 1)
Do not despise the words of prophets,
but test everything.
Hold fast to what is good,
and abstain from every form of evil.
As children of the light,
in all things bear testimony to the light,
that others may believe through you.

Call to Prayer (1 Thessalonians 5:16-19 NRSV)
Rejoice always, pray without ceasing, give thanks in all
circumstances; for this is the will of God for you in Christ
Jesus. Do not quench the Spirit, but in all things let your
prayers be made known to God. Let us pray.

THANKSGIVING AND COMMUNION

*Call to the Offering (Isaiah 61, Psalm 126,
1 Thessalonians 5)*
As those whom the God of peace has sanctified,
those whose hopes and dreams have been restored,
let us reflect the light we have been given.
May our offerings express our joy and exultation
for the gift of our salvation.
May our gifts to God reflect our wonder and gratitude
for being clothed in the garments of salvation
and the robes of righteousness. Amen.

SENDING FORTH

Benediction (Isaiah 61, Psalm 126,
1 Thessalonians 5:23-24)
    May the God of peace sanctify you completely.
    May the Christ of hope clothe you in the garments
       of salvation and the robes of righteousness.
    May the Spirit of joy turn your weeping into laughter.
    May your spirit and soul and body be kept sound
       and blameless at the coming of our Lord,
          Jesus Christ.
    The One who calls you is faithful and will do this.
    Go with God.

CONTEMPORARY OPTIONS

Gathering Words (Psalm 126)
    Dream on, people of God.
       We dream of a world filed with laughter—
       a world filled with cries of joy, not sorrow.
    Dream on, sisters and brothers in Christ.
       We dream of a world free of the chains
       that bind us—a world filled with shouts
       of thanksgiving, not anguish.
    Dream on, children of the Spirit.
       We worship a God who turns our dreams
       into reality.

Praise Sentences (John 1)
    Christ is our light.
       We rejoice in God's love.
    Christ is our light.
       We rejoice in God's salvation.
    Christ is our light.
       Christ is our light.
    Christ is our light.

DECEMBER 21, 2014

Fourth Sunday of Advent
Mary J. Scifres

COLOR
Purple

SCRIPTURE READINGS
2 Samuel 7:1-11, 16; Luke 1:47-55; Romans 16:25-27;
Luke 1:26-38

THEME IDEAS
God is in our midst, yearning to be at the center of our
worship and our lives. From ancient conversations with
Samuel and David to the Spirit's in-breaking into Mary's
young life, from the Pentecost miracle to the modern celebration of Christmas, God is in our midst. The Spirit is
breaking into our lives, and God is molding us to be a
household, not only of faith, but of love and justice. God
has looked with favor upon all who welcome God into
our midst. And God blesses us with the opportunity to be
and become the realm of God's presence here on earth.

INVITATION AND GATHERING

Call to Worship (Luke 1)
Let us magnify our God.
   We rejoice in the Savior among us!
God's mercy is upon us, God's strength is with us.

God's righteousness calls us to justice and peace.
Let us magnify our God.
We worship in spirit and love.

Opening Prayer (Luke 1)

Ever-present God,
we thank you for gathering us together
this day.
Send your Spirit to live within us,
that we may birth the Christ-child anew
this Christmas season.
Bless us to be your people—
a people of justice and love,
that the world may know your presence
and experience your saving grace.
With joy and hope, we pray. Amen.

PROCLAMATION AND RESPONSE

Prayer of Confession (Luke 1)

Look with favor upon us, O God,
even when we do not perceive your presence
in our lives.
Guide us to live as your household of faith,
even when we do not follow your path
of justice and love for all.
Have mercy upon us, Holy One:
forgive our pride, forgive our selfishness,
forgive our negligence, forgive us our sins.
Restore us to be your people,
and send your Spirit to live in and among us,
that we may bear the message of Christ's love
in all that we say and in all that we do. Amen.

Words of Assurance (Luke 1)

God has looked with favor on our low estate
and granted us favor.
The Christmas gift is ours, for Christ is with us:
forgiving and receiving us, even as we have forgiven
and received one another. Amen.

Passing the Peace of Christ (Luke 1)

As forgiven people made whole in Christ, let us receive one another with signs of peace and love.

Introduction to the Word (Romans 16, Luke 1)

The Holy Spirit is come upon us.
The Word of God is sent among us.
The mystery of God is revealed within us.
Listen, for God is speaking now.

Response to the Word or Prayer of Response (Luke 1)

We come to you, O God,
ready to be bearers of Christ to the world.
Send your Spirit into our very lives,
that we may be your servants of love.
Scatter the pride that would harden our hearts.
Fill us with your goodness and grace.
Strengthen us with your justice and righteousness.
Humble us with your mercy and compassion.
Make the impossible possible,
as we birth your realm of love in the world.
Let it be with us according to your word.

THANKSGIVING AND COMMUNION

Invitation to the Offering (Luke 1)

Bring your gifts, bring your lives, for none are barren here. God's Spirit dwells within us, and each of us bears gifts that are needed to bring Christ to the world. Come, let us give birth to new possibilities as we share God's gifts with a world in need.

Offering Prayer (Luke 1)

Dwell in us, Holy Spirit.
Dwell in these gifts,
    and transform them to be Christ's presence
        for all who are touched through these offerings.
In your holy name, we pray. Amen.

Communion Prayer (Luke 1)
Pour out your Holy Spirit on us,
  as you poured your Spirit into Mary's womb.
Pour out your Holy Spirit
  on these gifts of bread and wine,
    that they may nourish us with Christ's presence,
      and that we may bear Christ's presence
        for all to see.
Make us one with you,
  through the power of your Holy Spirit
    dwelling within us.
Make us one with one another,
  that we may be your household of faith.
Make us one in ministry with the world,
  that the hope of unity is made possible
    through your miraculous presence. Amen.

SENDING FORTH

Benediction (Luke 1)
God's Spirit has blessed us and goes forth with us now.
**We will bear Christ's loving presence
into the world.**
Lift up the lowly. Fill the hungry with good things.
We go to build God's realm here on earth.

CONTEMPORARY OPTIONS

Gathering Words (2 Samuel 7, Luke 1)
To a shepherd boy in the hills of Palestine,
  God called and dwelt in his midst.
To a poor girl in a house in Galilee,
  God called and dwelt in her midst.
To a boy in Lebanon, a girl in India,
  God calls and dwells in their midst.
To each of us here and the many who are not,
  God calls and dwells in our midst.
Come and worship, for God is with us now.

Praise Sentences (Luke 1)
O, magnify the Lord!
Sing of God's mercy and grace!
O, magnify the Lord!
Sing of God's mercy and grace!

DECEMBER 24, 2014

Christmas Eve
Mary Petrina Boyd

COLOR
White

SCRIPTURE READINGS
Isaiah 9:2-7; Psalm 96; Titus 2:11-14; Luke 2:1-20

THEME IDEAS
On this night, we hear Isaiah's promise of a child who will bring light, peace, justice, and righteousness. Psalm 96 summons all creation to sing for joy at the Lord's coming, for righteousness and truth shall mark God's realm. The epistle reflects on the theological meaning of the Incarnation: In Jesus we see God's grace and experience salvation. And Luke recounts the birth of Jesus. On this holy night: Isaiah speaks of peace, the psalmist sings of joy, Paul writes of peace, and Luke proclaims love incarnate.

INVITATION AND GATHERING

Call to Worship (Luke 2)
This is a night of deep mystery—
a night when heaven comes to earth.
This is a night of great love—
a night when a child is born for us.
This is a night of incredible joy—

a night when angels sing to shepherds.
Glory to God in the highest! Peace to all on earth.
O Come let us adore him, Christ the Lord!

Opening Prayer (Isaiah 9, Luke 2)

Incarnate One, Light of the World, Prince of Peace,
    draw close to us we pray.
In the darkness of this night,
    fill us with your light
        as we sing your message of peace
            with choirs of angels.
Open our eyes to love born anew.
Open our hearts to wonder at your love,
    that we may reflect your glory. Amen.

PROCLAMATION AND RESPONSE

Prayer of Confession (Titus 2)

Holy One, your grace has appeared among us;
    the light of your love has shined upon us.
Yet, instead of rejoicing in your light,
    we dwell in the darkness of despair,
        wearied from our many tasks,
            and burdened by the world's expectations.
Help us to be fully present to the miracle of this night,
    that we might see the beauty of your gift,
        find peace in your presence,
            and hear the song of the angels. Amen.

Words of Assurance (Isaiah 9, Titus 2)

The grace of God has appeared, bringing hope.
A child is born, bringing peace.
This is God's gift to us this night:
    a gift of forgiveness, a gift of peace,
    a gift of a new beginning.

Passing the Peace of Christ (Isaiah 9, Luke 2)

A child has been born for us,
    bringing endless peace to all people.

315

Glory to God in the highest heaven.
Peace to all on earth.

Introduction to the Word (Luke 2)

As these scriptures proclaim the ancient story of love, may we hear it anew. May we, like Mary, ponder all these things in our hearts.

Response to the Word (Luke 2 NRSV, Titus 2)

(For a children's service)
Thank you, God, for the story of love. Thank you for Mary and Joseph, who took care of baby Jesus. Thank you for the angels who told the good news of his birth. Thank you for the shepherds who came to see the baby born in a manger. And most of all, thank you for Jesus, who taught us that we should love one another. Amen.

(For other services)
The grace of God is here, born in Jesus Christ.
Having seen his glory, we rejoice,
    for he is our blessed hope, our news of great joy.
Unto us is born a Savior, the Messiah, the Lord.
With the angels we say: "Glory to God in the highest!"

THANKSGIVING AND COMMUNION

Invitation to the Offering (Isaiah 9, Luke 2)

The angels did not sing to kings in palaces. They came to poor shepherds tending sheep in the fields. May we give generously this night, in the hope that all may know justice and righteousness. May we give with joy, that God's realm of peace may come on earth.

Offering Prayer (Psalm 96, Luke 2)

God of blessing,
    you come to us in the gift of a child.
God of peace,
    you offer us good news of great joy.
We have heard the word;
    we have felt the joy.

As we bring our gifts of praise and thanksgiving,
we join with all creation in joyous wonder. Amen.

Great Thanksgiving (Isaiah 9, Luke 2)

Creating God, in the beginning was the Word.
You spoke the Word and the world came into being.
The Word you spoke was hope.
The Word you spoke was justice.
The Word you spoke was love.
Throughout the years the prophets echoed your Word,
promising a child who would bring light
to our darkness, a child who would bring
endless peace to our world of violence.
In the fullness of time, you sent your Word to us.
A child was born in a stable.
A star shone, leading the world to the child.
Angels came to shepherds
with good news and songs of praise.
There was great joy for all people,
for Jesus Christ was born:
savior of the world,
hope of the nations,
light for all creation.
The baby grew into a man who healed the sick,
reached out in compassion,
taught your ways,
and proclaimed your truth.
On his last night with his friends,
he gave us one more gift—
the gift of a meal for remembering;
the gift of a meal for hope and joy.
And so, Jesus took the bread,
gave thanks to you,
broke the bread, and gave it to his friends,
sharing the nourishment of body and spirit.
He said to them:
"Take, eat, and remember.
I am Emmanuel, God with you."

After supper Jesus took the cup,
    gave thanks to you, and shared it with his friends.
He said to them:
    "Drink this.
    This is a cup of blessing, a cup of forgiveness.
    This is God's gift, offered in love."
And so, we ask your blessing on these ordinary things:
    gifts of the earth, gifts of bread and fruit of the vine.
Make them be for us Jesus Christ,
    gift of love, Emmanuel, hope of the nations.
Send your Spirit upon us this night,
    that we may be the faithful body of Christ,
    sharing the gift of your love
    with grateful hearts and joyful minds.
Bless us this night and forevermore.

SENDING FORTH

Benediction (Isaiah 9, Luke 2, based on a poem by Howard Thurman)

Go forth to do the work of Christmas:
    Find the lost, heal the broken, feed the hungry,
    release the prisoner, rebuild the nations,
    bring peace among brothers and sisters,
    make music in the heart.
May the singing of the angels go with you.

—OR—

Benediction (Luke 2)

May the song of the angels delight you.
May the joy of the shepherds be yours.
May you ponder all these things, like Mary,
    in your hearts.
May God's peace be yours this holy night!
Go with haste to find the babe.

—OR—

Benediction (Luke 2)
> As you go forth into the darkness,
>   may the love of God light your way,
>   may the peace of God drench your souls,
>   and may the mystery of God's grace
>   surround you with joy.

CONTEMPORARY OPTIONS

Gathering Words (Luke 2)
> Come to Bethlehem this night.
> **There is something wonderful happening.**
> Come to the stable.
> **Mary and Joseph are there.**
> Come to the manger.
> **The baby Jesus is born.**
> Come out to the fields.
> **Hear the angels sing to shepherds.**
> Follow the star.
> **Come and see the baby.**

Praise Sentences (Isaiah 9, Psalm 96, Luke 2)
> Unto us a child is born.
> **Rejoice and be glad.**
> The light shines in the darkness.
> **Peace to all the world.**
> Let all creation rejoice.
> **A child is born for us.**
> Glory to God in the highest.
> **Peace to all on earth.**

DECEMBER 25, 2014

Christmas Day

B. J. Beu

COLOR

White

SCRIPTURE READINGS

Isaiah 52:7-10; Psalm 98; Hebrews 1:1-4, (5-12); John 1:1-14

THEME IDEAS

Although the birth of Jesus is the focus of Christmas, themes of grace and salvation flow from this event and shape today's scripture message. Our spirits need to sing and rejoice, not only today when we celebrate Christ's birth, but throughout the whole Christmas season, indeed throughout the whole year. This need is as ancient as the word of God itself. Allow the words and images of today's scriptures to inspire your services of worship, that everyone may glimpse the glory of this ancient miracle and feel its enduring power to transform our lives.

INVITATION AND GATHERING

Call to Worship (John 1, Psalm 98)

In the beginning was the Word,
and the Word was with God,
and the Word was God.
Make a joyful noise to the Lord, all the earth.

Let the seas roar and the mountains quake.
Everything came into being through the Word.
What came into being was life,
and the life was the light for all people.
Sing to the Lord a new song,
for God has done marvelous things.
The Word became flesh and blood,
and lived among us to bring all people to the light.
Let heaven and earth break forth
into joyous song, singing praises to our God.
The light shines in the darkness
and the darkness has not overcome it.
Christ, our light, shines forth in glory.
Christ, our life, brings us grace and truth.
Alleluia!

Opening Prayer (John 1)
God of life and light,
    as you awoke to the world
        on that Christmas morning
            so many years ago,
                awake in our lives today.
Teach us how to welcome the light,
    and believe in the power of the light
        to dispel the darkness,
            that we may be known
                as children of the light.
Shine the light of your love
    into every corner of the earth,
        that all who walk in darkness
            may behold the brightness
                of your dawn. Amen.

PROCLAMATION AND RESPONSE

Prayer of Confession (Isaiah 52, Hebrews 1)
God of new beginnings,
    long ago you spoke to our ancestors

through the words of the prophets,
 but now you speak to us
 through a Son.
Forgive us, Holy One,
 when we get lost in the trappings of this day:
 in the exchanging of gifts
 and the excess feasting at table
 with family and friends,
 forgetting to honor your Son
 as the reflection of your glory.
Focus our hearts on the reason for the season,
 that we may be messengers of peace
 and children of your Spirit. Amen.

Words of Assurance (Psalm 98, Hebrews 1)

Christ judges us with righteousness and equity,
 and loves us with grace and mercy.
Through the gracious gift of God,
 and the love of Christ, we are forgiven!

Passing the Peace of Christ (Isaiah 52)

How beautiful are the feet of the messenger who announces peace. How radiant are the eyes of the messenger who shines the light of God's love. May our feet be beautiful and our eyes radiant as we share signs of peace and words of love with one another.

THANKSGIVING AND COMMUNION

Offering Prayer (Hebrews 1, John 1)

God of light and love,
 bless our giving this Christmas Day
 and in the year ahead.
Send these offerings into the world
 on the wings of your angels,
 that those who are touched by our gifts
 may feel the warmth
 of your holy fire.

322

Shine in our lives
  and in our ministries,
    that the whole world may see
      your joyous light. Amen.

SENDING FORTH

Benediction (Isaiah 52, Psalm 98, John 1)
Make a joyful noise to the Lord.
We will sing praises to our God.
Walk in darkness no longer.
We will walk in the light of Christ.
Live with grace and joy.
We will be messengers of peace.
Go and proclaim the good news.
Jesus Christ is born. Alleluia!

CONTEMPORARY OPTIONS

Gathering Words (Isaiah 52, Psalm 98)
Make a joyful noise to the Lord.
Sing of laughter and love.
Break forth into joyous song.
Dance in utter ecstacy.
Proclaim the miracle of our Lord's birth.
Sing of hope and rebirth.

Praise Sentences (Psalm 98)
Glory to God in the highest!
Sing to the Lord a new song!
Go tell it on the mountain
that Jesus Christ is born!
Glory to God in the highest!
Sing to the Lord a new song!

DECEMBER 28, 2014

First Sunday after Christmas

Mary J. Scifres

COLOR

White

SCRIPTURE READINGS

Isaiah 61:10–62:3; Psalm 148; Galatians 4:4-7; Luke 2:22-40

THEME IDEAS

The glory of God's extraordinary salvation through Christ Jesus is juxtaposed with the ordinary, ritual presentation of a young Jewish boy at temple. Even as his family participates in this common custom, the uncommon breaks in. Simeon proclaims Jesus to be the long-awaited Messiah, the salvation for which Simeon has waited. Anna praises God for this young child, in whom she sees "the redemption of Jerusalem." Christmas is a reminder that our extraordinary God breaks into our ordinary world, our ordinary lives, and our ordinary traditions.

INVITATION AND GATHERING

Call to Worship (Isaiah 61–62, Psalm 148, Luke 2)
Rejoice with the heavens: Christ is born!
  God's light has come to earth.
Sing of this miracle: God's salvation is for all.
  We sing with all the earth!

Opening Prayer (Luke 2, Galatians 4)
    Light of the world,
        shine in our lives this day.
    As we hear your word and as we worship,
        help us grow in the strength and wisdom
            of your love.
    Bless us with the faith of Simeon and the hope of Anna,
        that we may find your miraculous presence
            in our worship and in our world.
    In your holy name, we pray. Amen.

PROCLAMATION AND RESPONSE

Call to Confession (Isaiah 61–62)
    Do not keep silent.
    Salvation in Christ comes like a burning torch.
    Already clothed in garments of salvation,
        let us confess our sins before our God.

Prayer of Confession (Isaiah 61–62, Galatians 4, Luke 2)
    Abba, Father, Spirit God,
        we yearn to be your children.
    Even in our yearning,
        we do not climb easily
            into your loving arms of grace;
        we do not wait patiently
            for your all-embracing presence;
        we do not trust persistently
            in your never-failing acceptance.
    Clothe us in the garland of your love,
        and adorn us in the jewels of your grace.
    Strengthen us with the roots of hope and faith,
        that we may be your children,
            and grow in wisdom and love
                all the days of our lives.

Words of Assurance (Isaiah 61–62, Galatians 4)
    Rejoice, sisters and brothers!
    Christ has clothed us with the garment of salvation.

We are covered with robes of righteousness.
We are adopted as children and heirs of God.
Christ is born is our lives.
God's love is with us now!

Passing the Peace of Christ (Galatians 4)
As children of God, we are sisters and brothers in Christ.
Let us share signs of peace with one another as the family
of God.

Prayer of Preparation (Galatians 4, Luke 2)
Shine on us with your wisdom, O God,
    as we listen and receive your word.
Let your word take root and grow in our lives,
    that we may be filled with your wisdom
        and your righteousness.
Let your Spirit rule in our hearts this day,
    that we may live as children
        who shine with your light and love.

Response to the Word (Luke 2)
Miraculous God,
    thank you for the extraordinary gift of Christmas.
Bless us with the faith of Simeon and the hope of Anna,
    that we may look for your miraculous presence
        in your extraordinary love,
            even as we live our ordinary lives.

THANKSGIVING AND COMMUNION

Invitation to the Offering (Luke 2)
When the time had come, Mary and Joseph brought Jesus
to the temple, dedicated him to God, and offered gifts to
God in thanksgiving and praise. In honor of that ancient
tradition, we come to this time of offering, dedicating ourselves to God and offering our own gifts of thanksgiving
and praise.

Offering Prayer (Luke 2)
Gracious God, thank you for these gifts
    and for the gift of your Son.

As we offer you these gifts,
  we also offer you our very lives.
Bless these gifts,
  that they may be signs
    of your redemption and your hope
      to a world in need.
Bless our lives,
  that we may shine with your glory,
    and light up the world with your love.
In Christ's name, we pray. Amen.

SENDING FORTH

Benediction (Isaiah 61–62, Luke 2)
  Go forth, no longer ordinary,
  but adopted into the family of God!
    **We go now to share the extraordinary news
    of Christ's birth and the truth of God's love,
    and hope for all the world!**

—OR—

Benediction (Isaiah 61–62, Luke 2)
  Go in peace, for we have seen the salvation of God.
    We go with joy, for Christ has clothed us with love.

CONTEMPORARY OPTIONS

Gathering Words (Luke 2)
  Even in an ordinary birth, in a humble stable,
  an extraordinary miracle occurred.
    We yearn for God's miracles today.
  Even in an ordinary religious tradition,
  prophets proclaimed Christ's extraordinary purpose.
    We yearn for God's miracles today.
  There is nothing ordinary about our extraordinary God.
    **There is nothing ordinary about our lives
    when we are guided by God's extraordinary Spirit.**

Ordinary miracles and extraordinary gifts
are all around us.
We yearn for God's miracles today.
Look and rejoice! God's miracles are all around.

Priase Sentences (Isaiah 61–62, Luke 2, Christmas)
Rejoice in Christ's birth, the miracle of life!
Rejoice and sing praise to God!
Rejoice in Christ's birth, the miracle of life!
Rejoice and sing praise to God!

CONTRIBUTORS

Laura Jaquith Bartlett, an ordained minister of music and worship, lives at a United Methodist retreat center in the foothills of Oregon's Mt. Hood, where she serves as the program director.

B. J. Beu (series co-editor) is senior pastor of Neighborhood Congregational Church in Laguna Beach, California. A graduate of Boston University and Pacific Lutheran University, Beu loves creative worship, preaching, and advocating for peace and justice.

Mary Petrina Boyd is pastor of Langley United Methodist Church on Whidbey Island. She spends alternating summers working as an archaeologist in Jordan.

Joanne Carlson Brown is the clergy-type for Tibbetts United Methodist Church in Seattle, Washington. She is also an adjunct professor at Seattle University School of Theology and Ministry and lives in Seattle with Thistle, the wee Westie.

Karin Ellis is a United Methodist pastor who lives in Tustin, California, with her husband and two children.

Safiyah Fosua is the assistant professor of Christian Ministry and Christian Worship at Wesley Seminary at Indiana Wesleyan University and a former staff member of the General Board of Discipleship for The United Methodist Church.

Rebecca J. Kruger Gaudino, a United Church of Christ minister in Portland, Oregon, teaches world religions and biblical studies as Visiting Professor at the University of Portland and also writes for the Church.

Jamie D. Greening is a husband, father, pastor, writer, and blogger who lives and ministers in Port Orchard, Washington.

Hans Holznagel served in communication, mission interpretation, and administrative and fundraising roles in the national ministries of the United Church of Christ from 1984 to 2011. He is now on the staff of Near West Theatre in Cleveland, Ohio, where he and his family are members of Archwood United Church of Christ.

Bill Hoppe is the music coordinator for Bear Creek United Methodist Church in Woodinville, Washington, and is a member of the band BrokenWorks, for which he is the keyboardist. He thanks his family and friends for their continued love, support, and inspiration.

Amy B. Hunter is a poet and Episcopal layperson who enjoys sitting in the pew after a decade of being part of a parish staff. She has discovered that writing is like prayer, both challenging and rewarding beyond description. Two outcomes of her writing life are "A Table in the Wilderness," available at Lulu.com, and the blog "Astrolabe and Trope" (http://astrolabeandtrope.wordpress.com/).

John Indermark is a United Church of Christ minister and writer who lives in the southwest corner of Washington state.

Sharon McCart was born and raised in California. The granddaughter and daughter of Methodist pastors, Sharon was not called to ministry until the age of 50. Ministry is her fourth career, following time as an R&D chemist, a full-time mom, and a special education teacher. She also loves to travel, to read, to garden, and to go on mission trips.

Matthew J. Packer is a United Methodist deacon serving as music director at Flushing United Methodist Church and as Small Membership Church consultant with the Crossroads District United Methodist Church. He is also choral director for Mott Community College and part of the music ministry duo Brother 2 Brother.

J. Wayne Pratt is a retired United Methodist pastor living in Wake Forest, North Carolina. A graduate of Syracuse University and Drew Theological School, Wayne enjoys writing liturgy, preaching, reading, and gardening.

Mary J. Scifres (series co-editor) serves as a consultant in leadership, church and culture, worship, and evangelism from her Laguna Beach home, where she and her spouse B. J. reside with their teenage son, Michael. Her books include *The United Methodist Music and Worship Planner, Prepare!,* and *Searching for Seekers.*

Deborah Sokolove is assistant professor of Art and Worship at Wesley Theological Seminary, where she also serves as director of the Henry Luce III Center for the Arts and Religion.

Terri Stewart is a graduate of Seattle University with a Master of Divinity and serves in ministry with the Youth Chaplaincy Coalition. You can find her at www.cloakedmonk.com.

Leigh Anne Taylor is the minister of music at Blacksburg United Methodist Church and lives with her family in the mountains of southwest Virginia. She has recently published a book that she co-wrote with her former husband, the Rev. Joe Cobb, *Our Family Outing: A Memoir of Coming Out and Coming Through.*

SCRIPTURE INDEX

Page numbers in italics refer to the online-only material.

COMMUNION PRAYER AND LITURGIES INDEX

In order of appearance